Mary Ellen Mark

Introduction by Caroline Bénichou

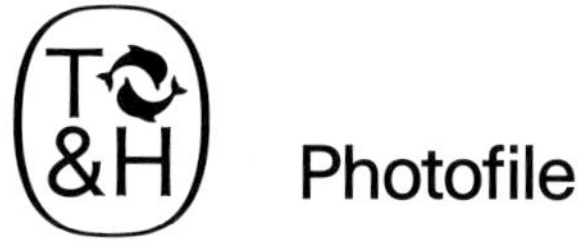

Photofile

A photographic odyssey

From circus acrobats to Hollywood stars, brothels to psychiatric hospitals, India to America—from the day she began taking photographs, Mary Ellen Mark brought her singular gaze to bear on the world around her. Photograph and photographer alike depend on the visible. Without a point of reference, there is no image: it is created from the concurrence of subject, camera, and photographer. Every photographer needs to forge (a process that involves coincidence as well as coexistence) a path through reality, whatever the cost. Mary Ellen Mark's way of understanding the world is, above all, an understanding of other human beings. Throughout her work, what seems particularly striking is how closely, how intimately, she connects with the people she photographs. She is not trying to draw attention to the exotic, the extraordinary, or the monstrous. Nothing especially eventful. Simply the experience—constantly repeated, always new—of the presence of another human being going about their daily life, observed within their social context, arrested in time by the still image, captured in two dimensions by the photograph.

Mary Ellen Mark's work is difficult to categorize: labels do not fit because she was always on the borderline of reportage, documentary photography, and portraiture. We might venture to call her a "social portraitist." It could also be said that her singular approach to tackling reality, and her mingling of different photographic genres, are what make her images so magnetic.

After graduating from the University of Pennsylvania's Annenberg School for Communication in 1964 with a masters

in photojournalism, Mark traveled to Turkey on a Fulbright
Scholarship. Already, a clear and lasting aspiration was emerging:
a desire to confront the other, via the raw process of imagemaking,
but with delicacy. She thus embarked on a photographic career that
would steer her toward other people in a way that demonstrated
an astonishing capacity to integrate herself into their worlds,
a diversity of social settings that she explored and decoded.

Ward 81   On her return to the United States, Mary Ellen Mark
combined her own personal projects with the commissions that
she received. Her images were published in major magazines such
as Life and *The New York Times*. She was also a set photographer for
several films (including *Fellini Satyricon*) and went on to work on
Milos Forman's *One Flew Over the Cuckoo's Nest*. It was through Forman
that she was introduced to Ward 81, the maximum security women's
ward at Oregon State Hospital, where the film was being shot. The
following year, in 1976, Mark and her friend, writer Karen Folger
Jacobs, obtained permission not simply to photograph the ward
but also to live in an adjacent, empty ward. The result was a moving
project that would generate a book and an exhibition entitled *Ward 81*.

Mental illness is viewed here from the inside, with no sense of
voyeurism, but instead confinement, vulnerability, violence, failure.
Women, young and old, with empty eyes, twisted hands, suffering
bodies. The expressions on gaunt faces seem menacing, almost bestial.
Alternatively, they betray distress, fear, bewilderment. Sometimes
there's a sense of calm. These images speak of lack and loss: loss of
freedom, altered states of mind, physical neglect, alienation. Mark
appears to have been fully present in this environment, to have
taken stock of all its rules and irregularities. She goes beyond simply
presenting the status quo; her work does more than merely observe
or demonstrate "this is what insanity is." Instead, she confronts
mental illness unflinchingly, engages with it it up close. And these
images constitute a challenge, for photographer and viewer alike:
by highlighting their humanity, the pictures force us to look at
these women as fellow human beings. With these raw, shocking,
witty photographs, stripped of any lewdness, Mary Ellen Mark

demonstrates her ability to enter a difficult, potentially impenetrable environment, and give the viewer a real sense of what that environment looks and feels like.

During the same period, however, Mark was also photographing celebrities and film stars. In 1977 she joined Magnum Photos (which she would leave in 1981). She gained both public recognition and professional acclaim. She brought the same focus to the marginalized, the mentally ill, and the big names of Hollywood—the gulf was not impassable. She had no problem moving between these very different worlds: for Mark, what remained a constant was the importance of getting close to her subjects, the photographic encounter.

Her fascination with India, which she first visited in 1968, demonstrated once again this ability to cross not only geographic but also social and cultural boundaries in order to grasp and share the lives of her fellow humans.

Falkland Road   Shimmering colors. Crimson fabrics flaming against electric blue walls. Bodies, slenderly built, voluptuous, amber-skinned. Beautiful women, some indifferent, some lascivious, some languid. Faces darkly glowering, or melancholy. We might be describing a distant, enchanted land, a sensual fantasy full of carnal delights. In fact, this is Falkland Road, a bustling thoroughfare in Mumbai where brothels sit cheek by jowl and women's bodies are bought and sold for a handful of rupees.

On each of her trips to India, Mary Ellen Mark wandered up and down Falkland Road, attempting to take photographs and to blend into the bustling life of the street. She was met with hostility from both the women and their clients, with buckets of water and garbage. Mark returned on multiple occasions, at first without success. Then, in 1978, she finally succeeded in mollifying her aggressors, eliciting a degree of curiosity and, little by little, winning over the women's trust. The people she encountered in Falkland Road included *hijras*, sex workers of all ages, girls who had been kidnapped and sold to the madams, young women from poor families who had been sold by their mothers. Many of them were still children. She met street girls—the most independent of the bunch—who worked without pimps but were robbed or beaten by their lovers, who were often pickpockets. She met "cage girls," who would beckon to clients with a repertoire of obscene gestures. And she gained access to the brothels where prostitutes and their children lived together and mothers operated as madams, in a manner both maternal and tyrannical, holding the reins.

The images are very raw, like those of the women with their clients. They reveal, and denounce, an unbearable level of hardship. The women are like idols from a rundown temple, lifted from the miniatures of a nightmarish Kama Sutra, at once sublime and pitiful. The photographer records their words, such as those of Munni, a fifteen-year-old sex worker: "The name tattooed on my arm is the only thing I can bring with me to my death." This is, of course, a piece of photojournalism on prostitution, but it is more than just an eyewitness account. Through the gaze she casts on them and the interest she devotes to them, Mary Ellen Mark perceives these sex workers with dignity, respecting their identity and humanity. She knows how to utilize sensitivity without condescending or wallowing in misery.

Each photograph reveals its silence and its secret, operating as an endless threshold for the viewer's gaze, a window onto possibilities that are unspoken but nevertheless present. Each photograph—we are given to understand—contains a drama that is gradually being played out. These women who have nothing but their bodies, these women who are treated as nothing but genitals for hire, gain an identity, a concrete—and shattering—human reality. Because we now know a little of their story and their lives.

Indian Circus   The latent mystery of the image and its quasi-theatrical quality can also be found in the photographs of traveling circuses that Mary Ellen Mark took, again in India, during a six-month period between 1989 and 1990 (in 1980, she had worked on a lengthy photo-essay focusing on Mother Teresa). Like the brothels of Mumbai, these circuses were a microcosm of wider society and offered Mark an ideal opportunity for observing humanity.

Traveling circuses are a world of strange and fantastical creatures. Faces caked in makeup, some silly, some solemn. White rabbits popping out of hats. Trained birds towing mysterious cargoes. Young girls with bodies like snakes, pliable, sinuous, twisting like vines into impossible contortions. Calm trainers of wild and exotic beasts.

A dwarf in clown makeup, with a hat crammed on his head, and extraordinarily tiny feet, passes before the camera lens. In his arms, a plump young boy, half naked, with dark-lashed eyes, is gently touching the man's cheek with a small hand (the man is his father, the caption tells us). Behind him, in the background, we get a glimpse of what appears to be a patched circus tent. Between the tent and the man is a path, not a very long path, but a path nevertheless. And we gather that he has walked the length of it—this fragile human being who carries—delicately, tenderly—the child, as beautiful as a temple idol, a son who seems to be his exact opposite, who weighs so heavily in his father's arms and serves to emphasize his short stature. This fascinating image merges adversity and grace.

While the circus is a commonplace theme in photography, Mary Ellen Mark succeeded in restoring its emotional charge without making it merely picturesque. The circus is a wonderfully old-fashioned and somewhat absurd phenomenon (like many other subjects that attracted Mark). It stands outside time, a sum of contradictions. The photographer takes us to the other side of the mirror, to a country of dreamlike marvels where ugliness goes hand in hand with fairytale enchantment, poverty with humour, and everything tends toward excess. Every circus is a closed realm, a world within a world. It is a highly concentrated community of unusual people, and as such it offers fascinating possibilities for the photographer to explore. And, in Mark's case, it was an experience she repeated by photographing circuses in Vietnam and Mexico.

It was not the spectators that interested her but the animals and the performers—the "actors," in other words. Actors is a fitting word because these men and women live much of their lives in the spotlight and the gap between life and performance is tenuous, the boundaries blurred: the extraordinary exists in place of the ordinary and we are never quite sure when the show is over.

Curiously enough, many photographs that Mark shot in the USA also depict people caught up in the world of performance, the world of spectacle—albeit a very different sort of spectacle. Once again, there were boundaries to be crossed and a route to be negotiated that would connect radically different worlds, with—as always in Mark's work—human beings as the link.

American Odyssey   The myth of America has been around, it seems, for a very long time, fuelled by images, movies, and consumer goods flooding out of the USA. And each of us carries inside our own heads, however laughable or closely guarded, our own American dream. We can see a foreshadowing of this insidious fascination with all things American in the Declaration of Independence: "We hold these truths to be self-evident, that all men are created equal, that they are endowed by their Creator with certain unalienable Rights, that among these are Life, Liberty, and the pursuit of Happiness." The New World versus the Old. Happiness elevated to the status of a right which, it seems, every American can claim. Mary Ellen Mark spent more than thirty years traveling back and forth across the USA, and wherever she went, she appears to have found signs of this same quest, overt or otherwise, for legitimate happiness, seemingly at any price. And, in her images, while the aspiration is palpable, access to the American Way is often another matter entirely. As Tiny remarked in the film *Streetwise*: "I wanna be really rich and live on a farm with a bunch of horses, which is my main best animal, and have three yachts or more and diamonds and jewels and all that stuff." Eighteen years later, she was on welfare, with five children by five different fathers … but still hopeful. She still had the right to search, to falter, to keep trying.

While not directly scrutinizing its failings, Mary Ellen Mark's photographs reveal the fakery of the American Dream by whisking us behind the scenes—to the edge of pathos, where poverty and despair go hand in hand with spangles and sequins. Mark's photographs are littered with society's rejects, sex workers, the mentally ill, gigolos, and musclemen, providing a fascinating and composite portrait of a stumbling, disenchanted America. A large woman in a fancy outfit has her face greedily licked by a tiny dog.

Families pose in squalid apartments. A provocative young girl, wearing a bikini and too much makeup, stands smoking a cigarette in a wading pool. This American odyssey is less of an expedition than the story of the human condition.

The gaze that Mary Ellen Mark brought to bear on her fellow human beings clearly reflects the respect she showed to those with whom she crossed paths. Her images are uncompromising, and it is in this rawness that their delicacy ultimately resides. While ruthless (though never gratuitously cynical), Mark was not without compassion. The time she devoted to Tiny, to the sex workers of Mumbai, and to the majority, in fact, of her photographic subjects, demonstrates the profound humanity that motivated her. Mary Ellen Mark was unquestionably a *woman* photographer. As she said herself, it was because she was a woman that she was able to gain the consent of the people she photographed, that they were willing to surrender themselves and set aside any feelings of shame, in a way that may well have been denied to a man. It was also thanks to her ability to set aside her own ego, to blend in and be accepted by the milieus which she photographed. Neither moralizing, nor biased, she knew how to create an emotional response that was free of sentimentality.

Photography is always a form of confrontation, of hostage-taking, an act of violence toward the subject, because the face-to-face nature of the encounter is betrayed by the presence of the camera. Mark fed on reality insatiably, but at no point did she act like a predator. She said that she only ever started taking photographs after approaching her subjects. There were no stolen images. Anyone who agreed to appear in front of the camera understood the deal. There was no abuse, no trap, no trickery.

For Mary Ellen Mark, this was as crucial for Indian sex workers as for wealthy Americans. The humanity shines through each of her images: unsettling, repugnant, harrowing, touching, absurd. And it was this same humanity that enabled Mark to connect with others by overcoming their "otherness," yet always avoiding the pitfalls of the cliché and the purely picturesque. What she demonstrated was an ability to understand people instinctively, regardless of their

cultural background, lifestyle, religion, or condition. She grasped and
conveyed to the viewer the fierce human will to survive, as expressed
within a particular social context (circus, brothel, medical clinic).
She was able, in her photographs, to reveal moments of grace and
uncover cruel paradoxes, critique forms of behavior that are laughable
or deplorable, and demonstrate how every person, through their
attitude, tends to be present within the image they project. What
stands out, invariably, is the other. The other for each of us, like
another self, an ephemeral other. And if Mary Ellen Mark's images
elicit unease, fascination, pity, or derision, if they unsettle us, it is
because they are a mirror in which the photographer invites us to see
our own reflection. Mary Ellen Mark's photographic odyssey leads
her, ultimately, to say something about the human condition itself.

Caroline Bénichou

1. Hippopotamus and performer,
Great Rayman Circus, Chennai, 1989.

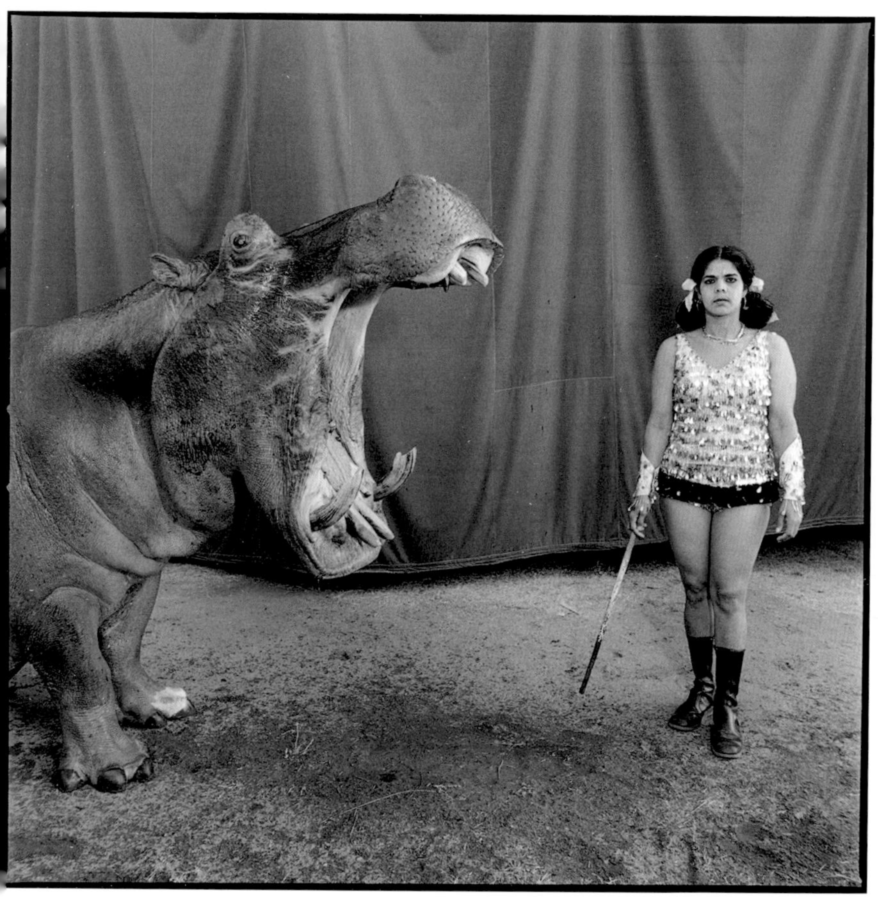

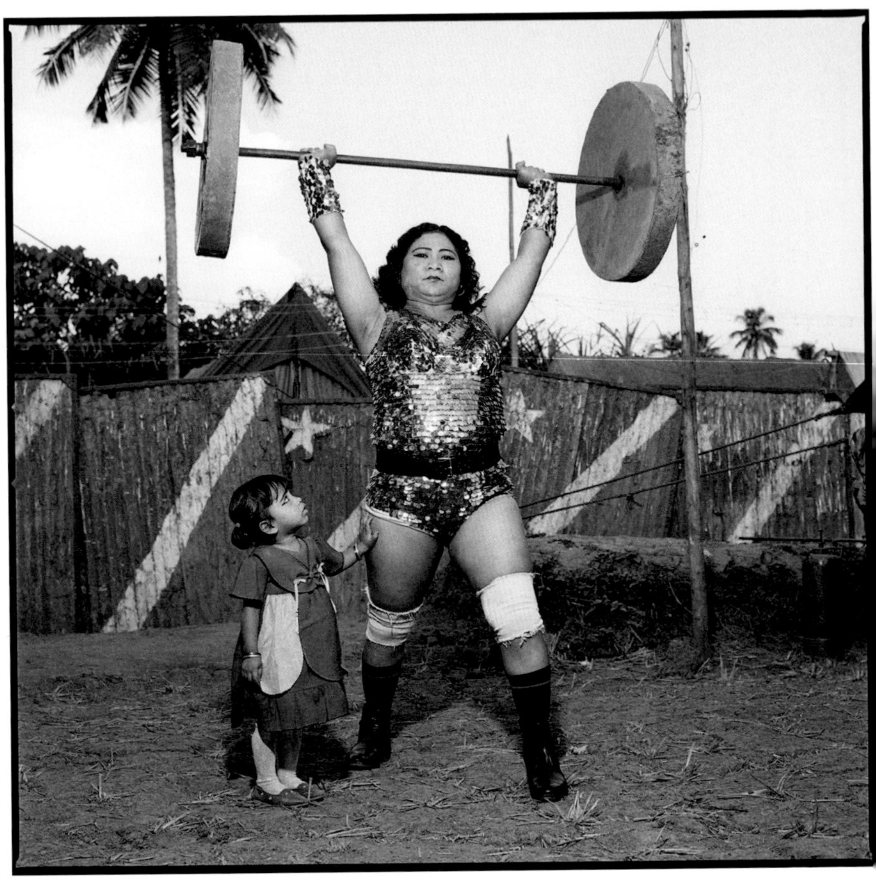

2. Shavanaas Begum with her three-year-old daughter,
Parveen, Gemini Circus. Perinthalmanna, India, 1989.

3. Jyotsana riding on Vahini, the elephant,
Amar Circus, Delhi, 1989.

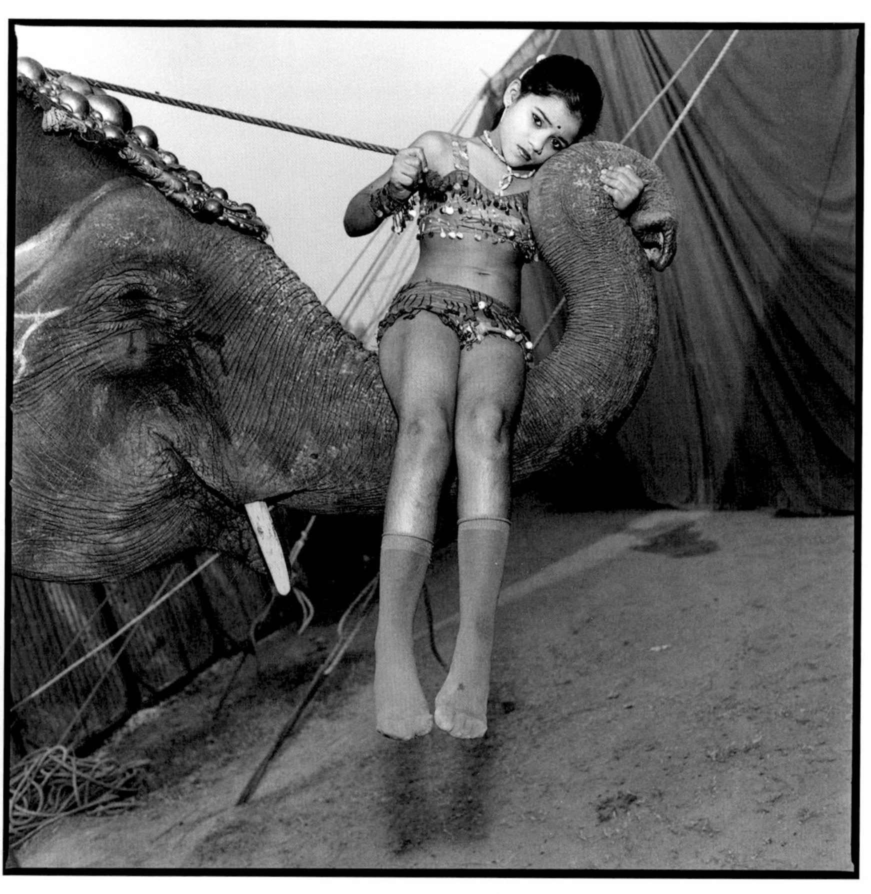

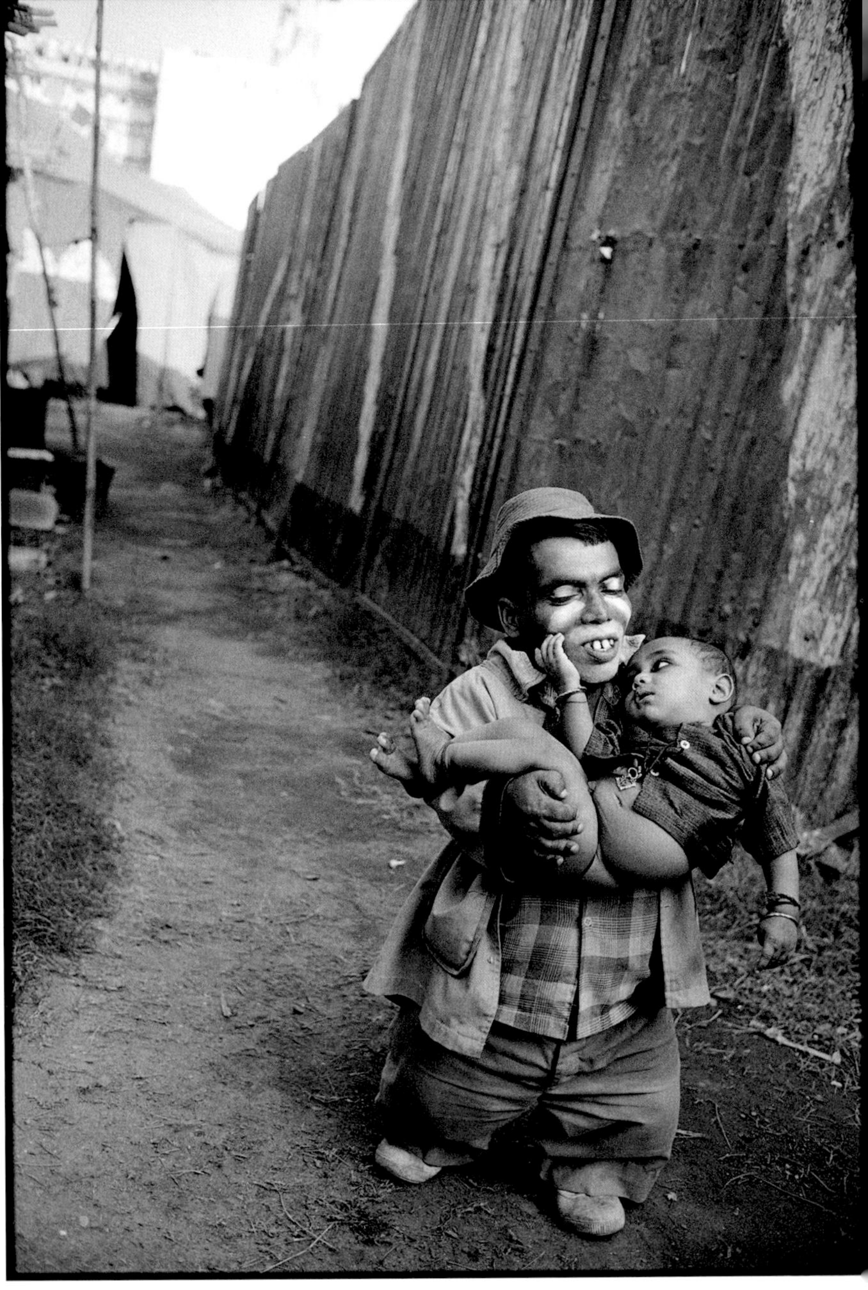

4. Usman of the Jumbo Circus,
carrying his son. Mumbai, 1992.

5. Ram Prakash Singh with his elephant, Shyama,
Great Golden Circus. Ahmedabad, India, 1990.

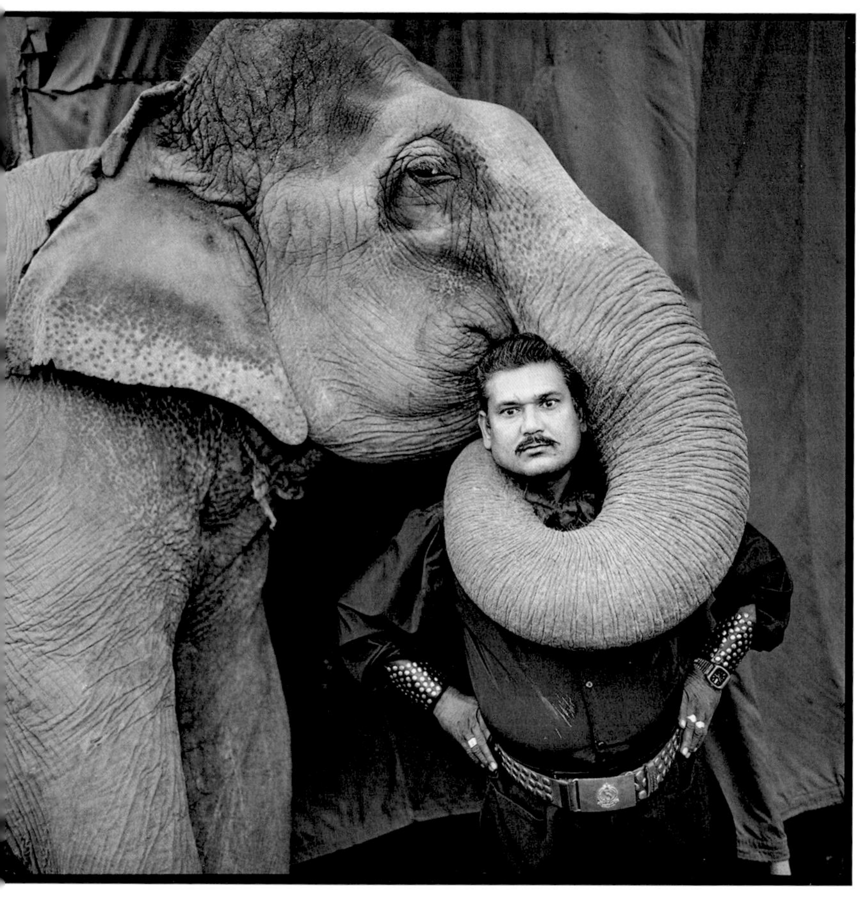

6. Kamla behind curtains with a customer.
Falkland Road, Mumbai, 1978.

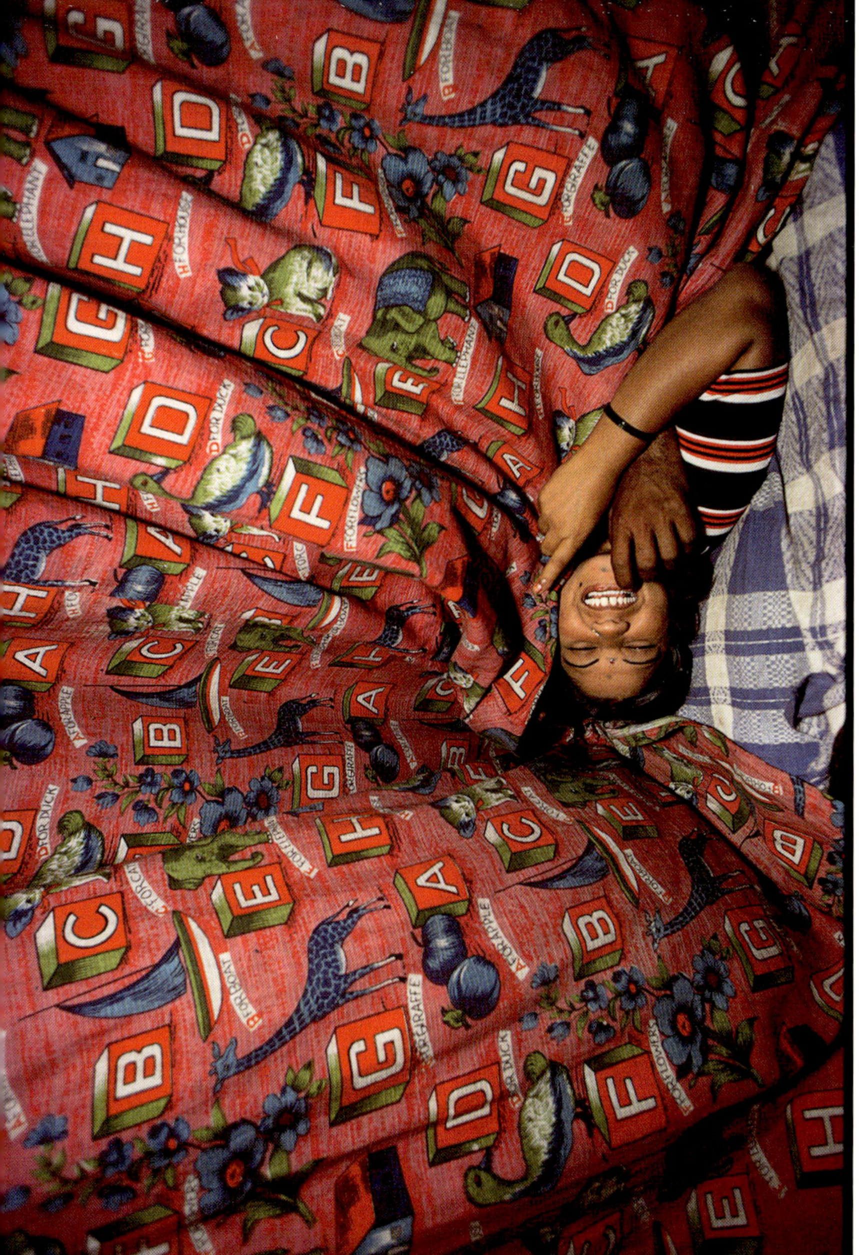

7. Chess by the beach. Sochi, Georgia, 1987.

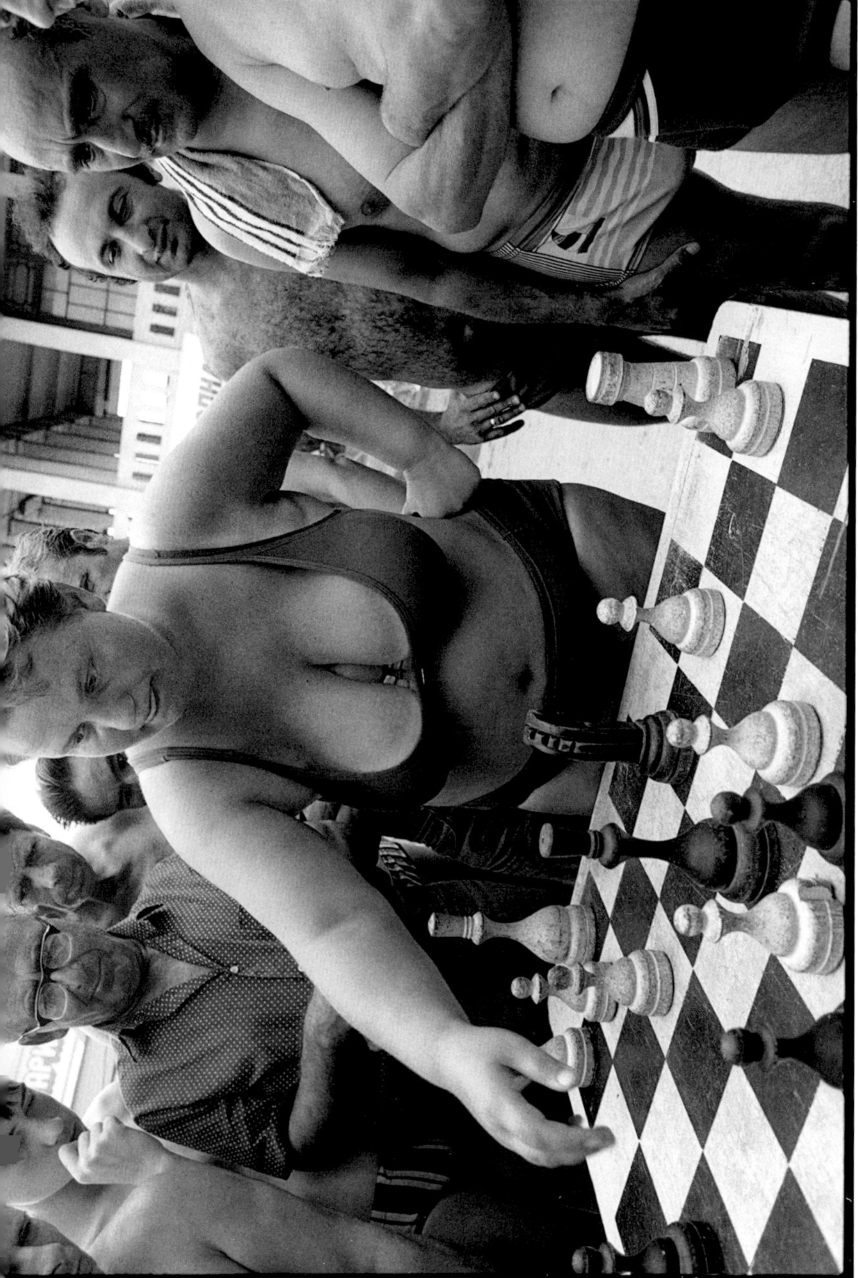

8. J'Lisa with a starfish. Seattle, 2014.

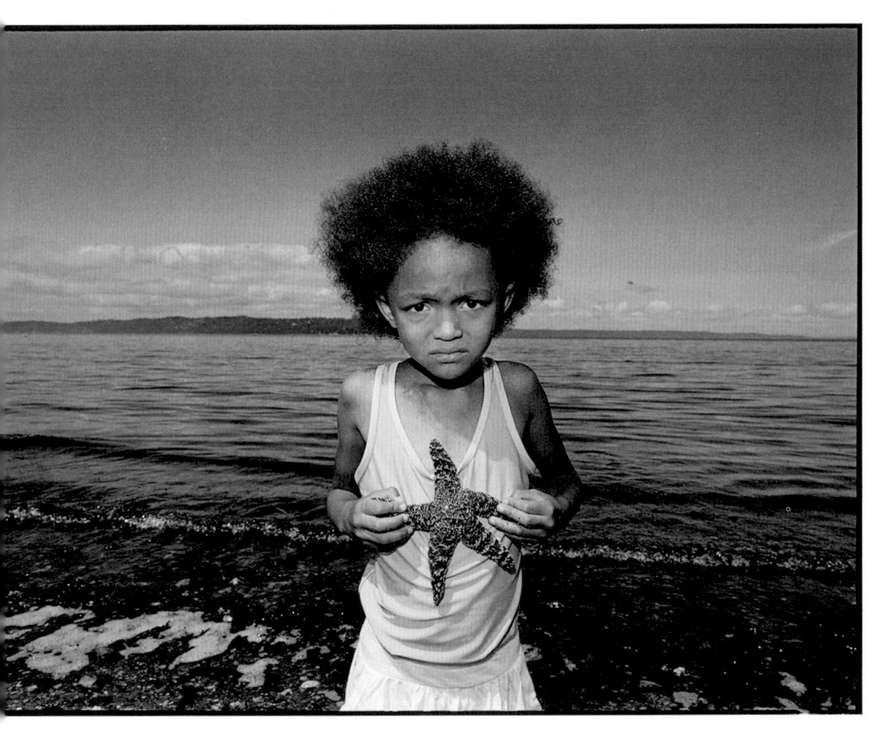

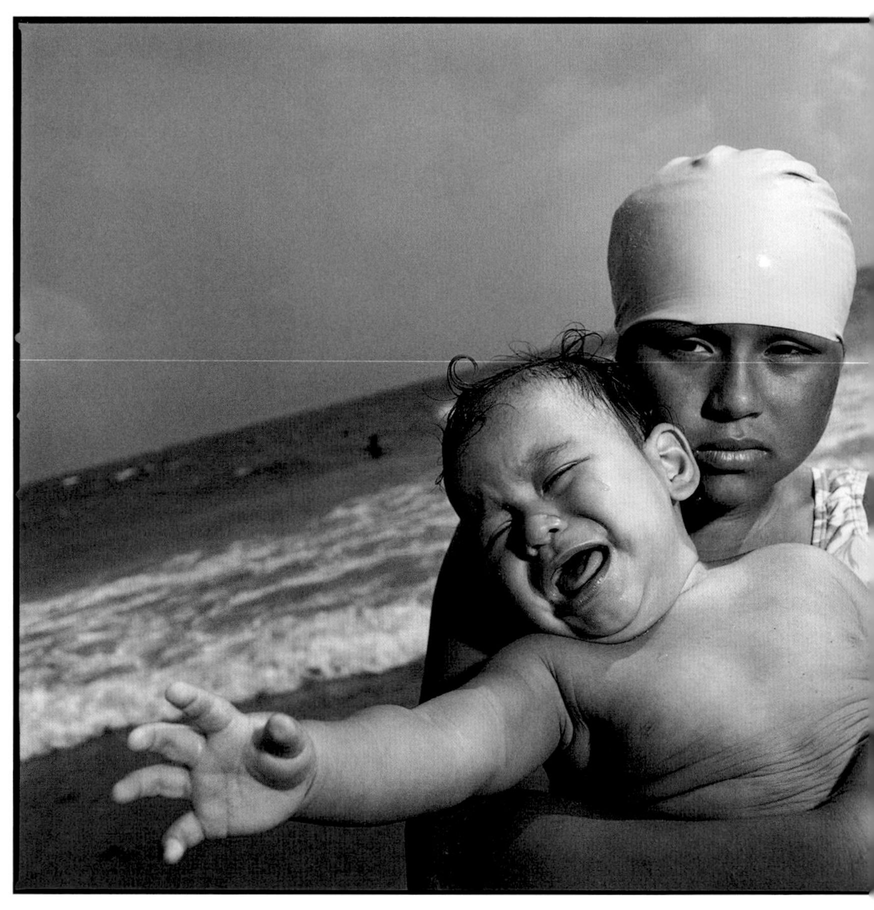

9. Girl and baby on the beach. Coney Island, New York, 1994.

10. Girl on the beach. Coney Island, New York, 1994.

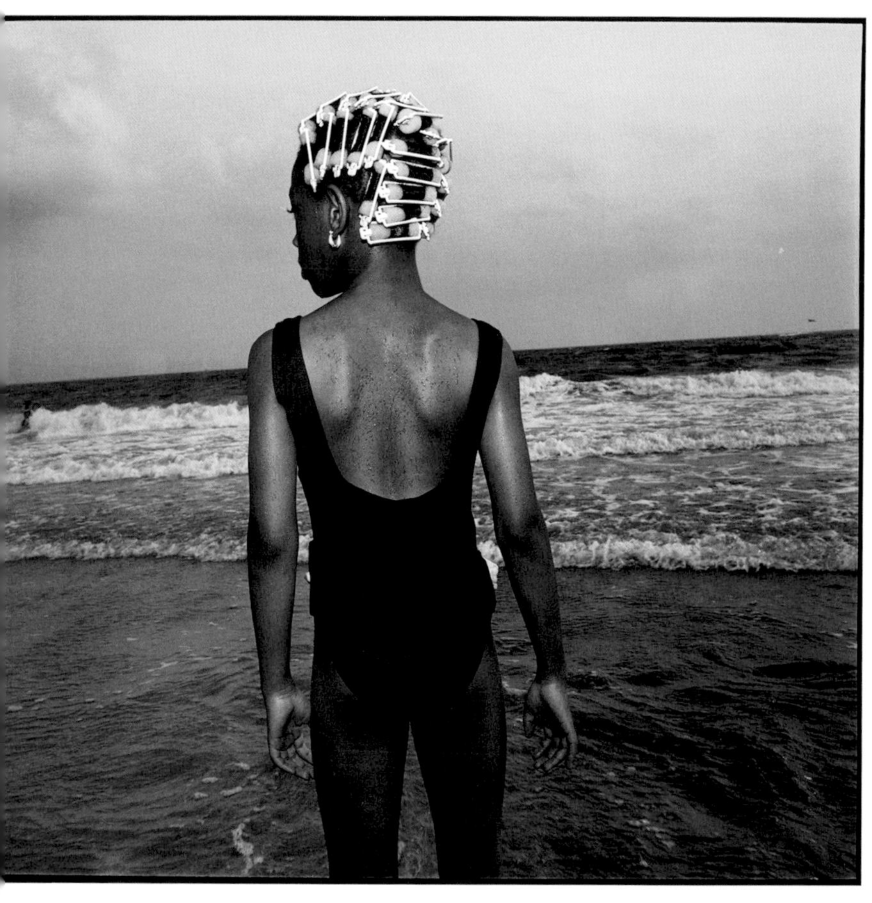

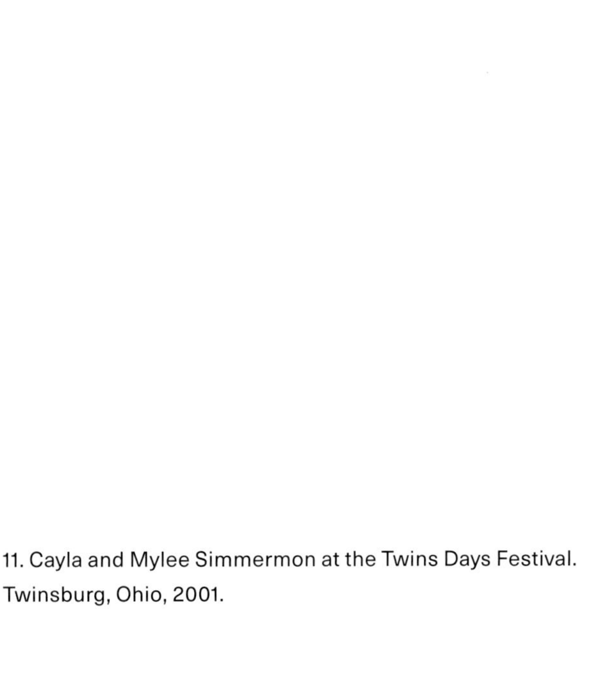

11. Cayla and Mylee Simmermon at the Twins Days Festival.
Twinsburg, Ohio, 2001.

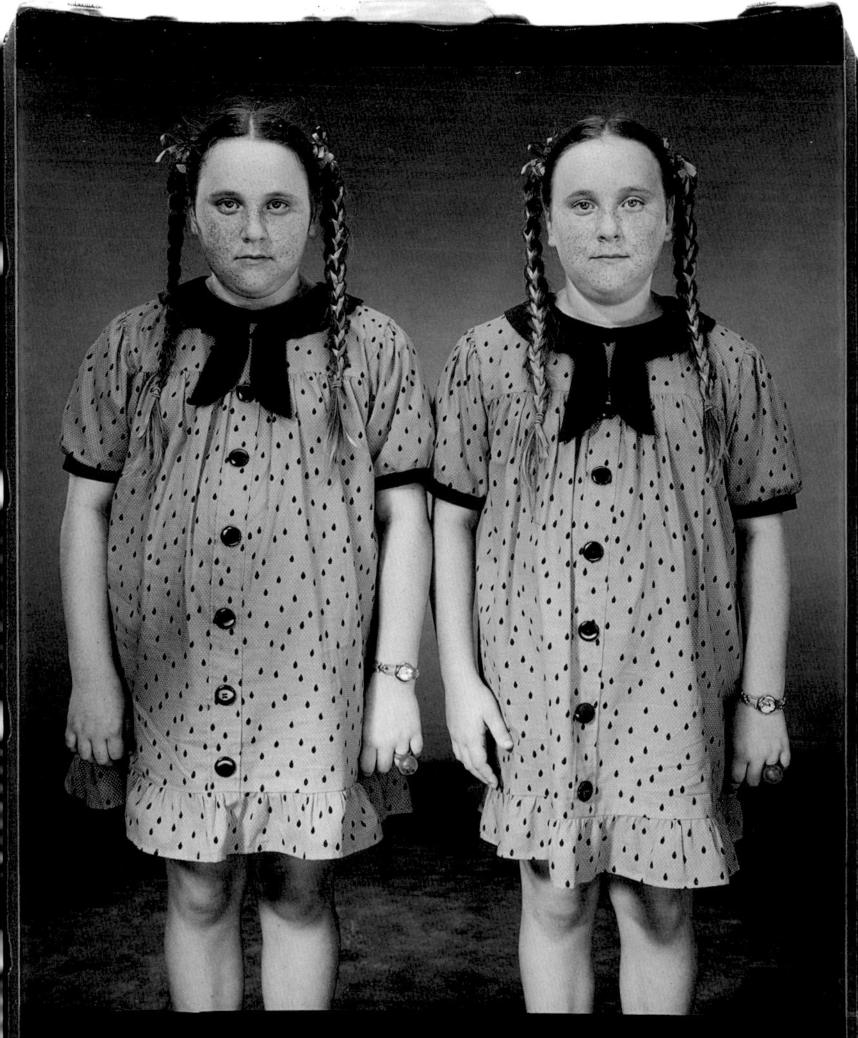

12. Emine dressed up for Republic Day.
Trabzon, Turkey, 1965.

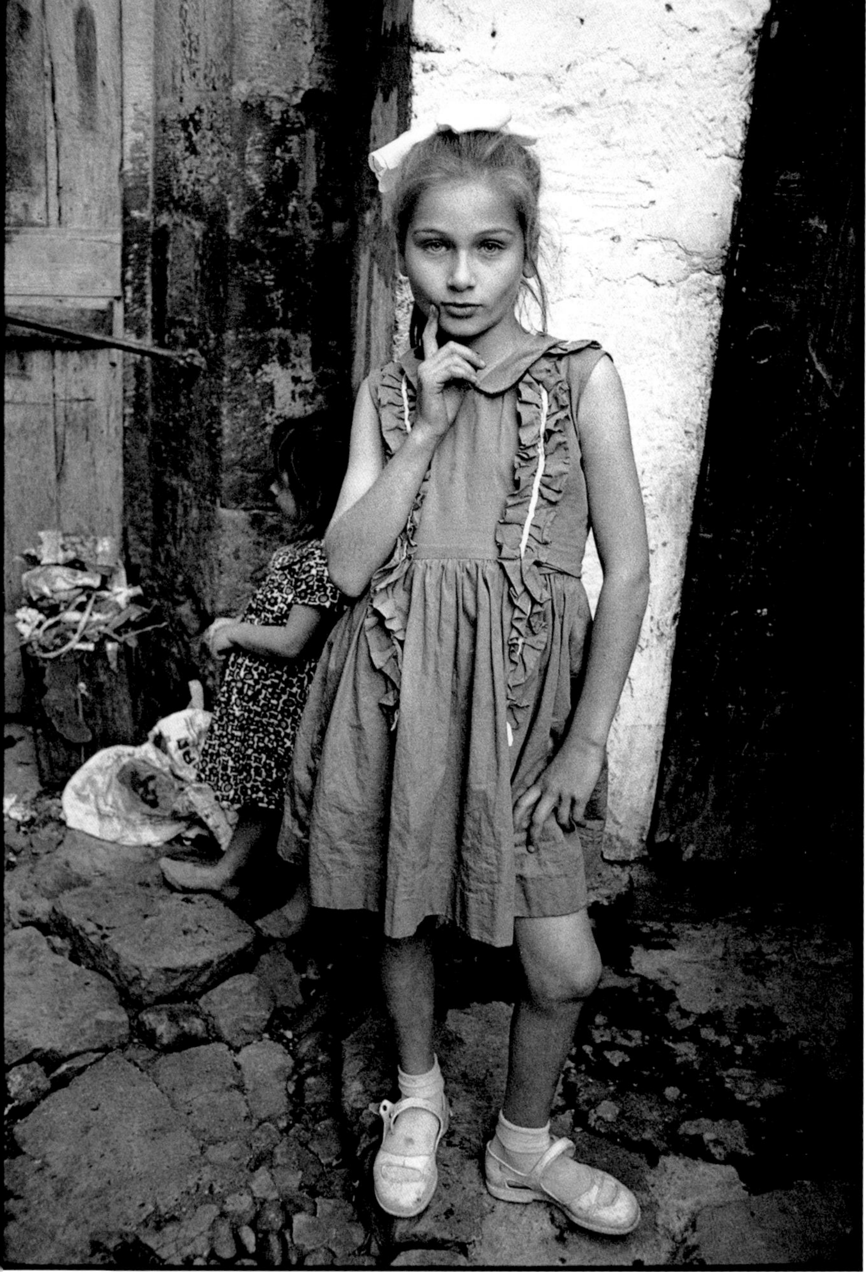

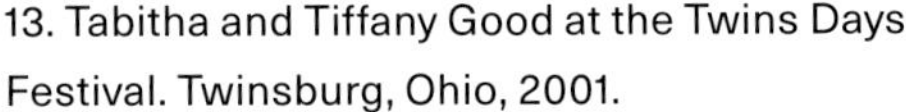

13. Tabitha and Tiffany Good at the Twins Days
Festival. Twinsburg, Ohio, 2001.

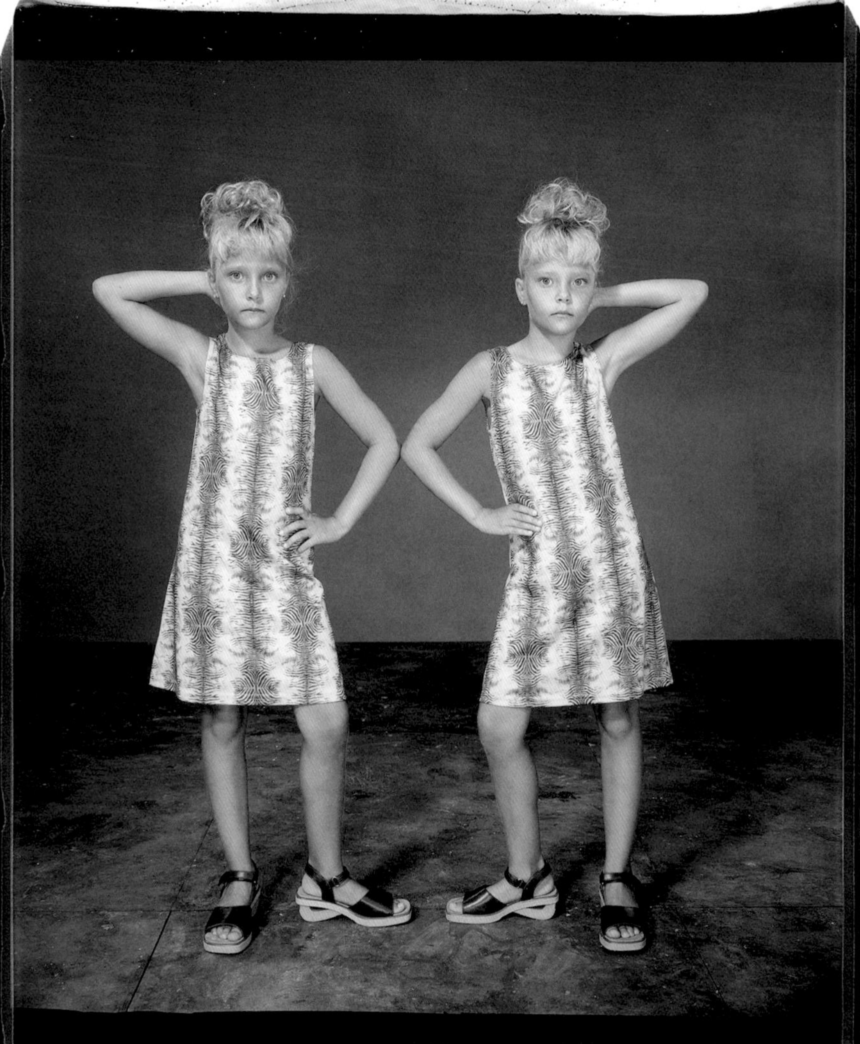

14. Laurie in the bathtub of Ward 81,
Oregon State Hospital. Salem, Oregon, 1976.

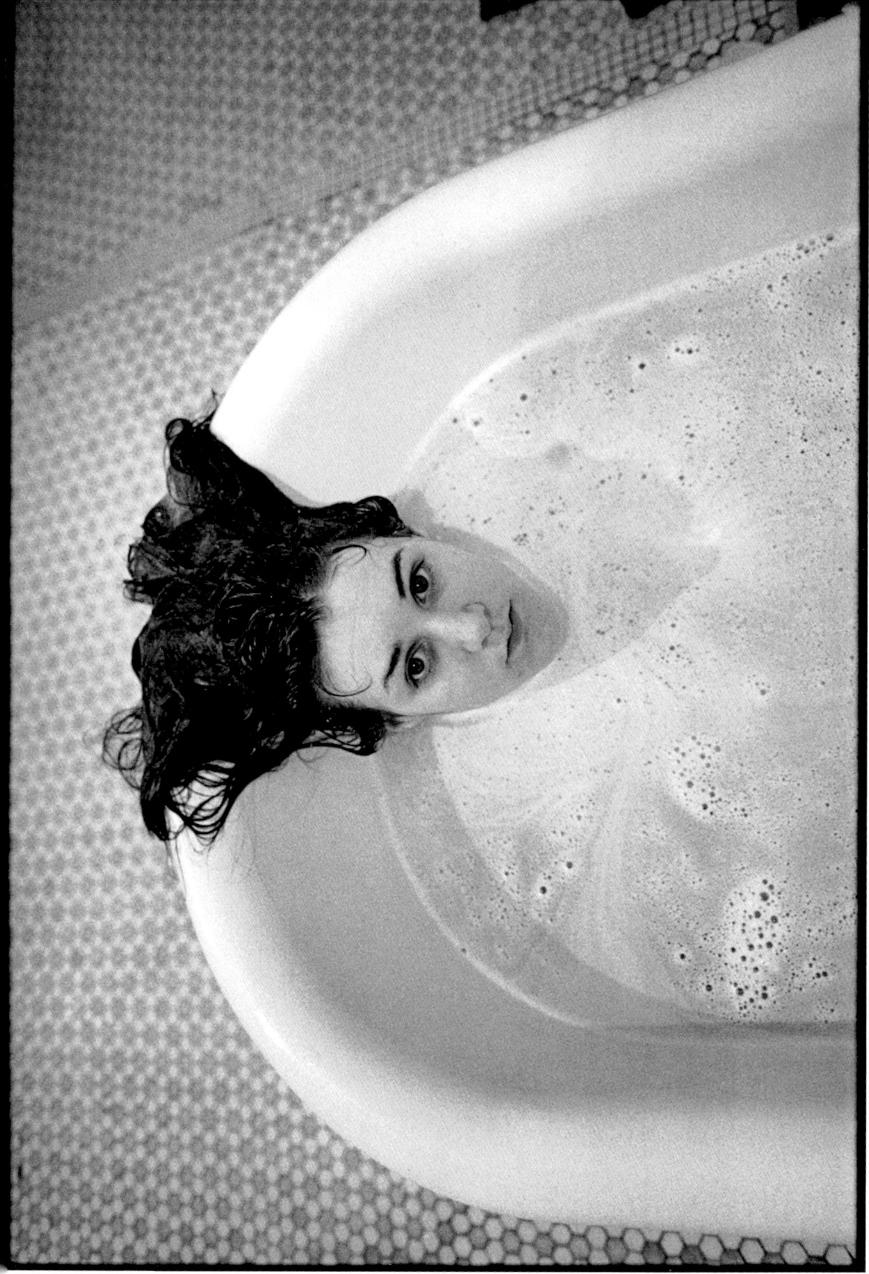

15. Mona, Ward 81, Oregon State Hospital.
Salem, Oregon, 1976.

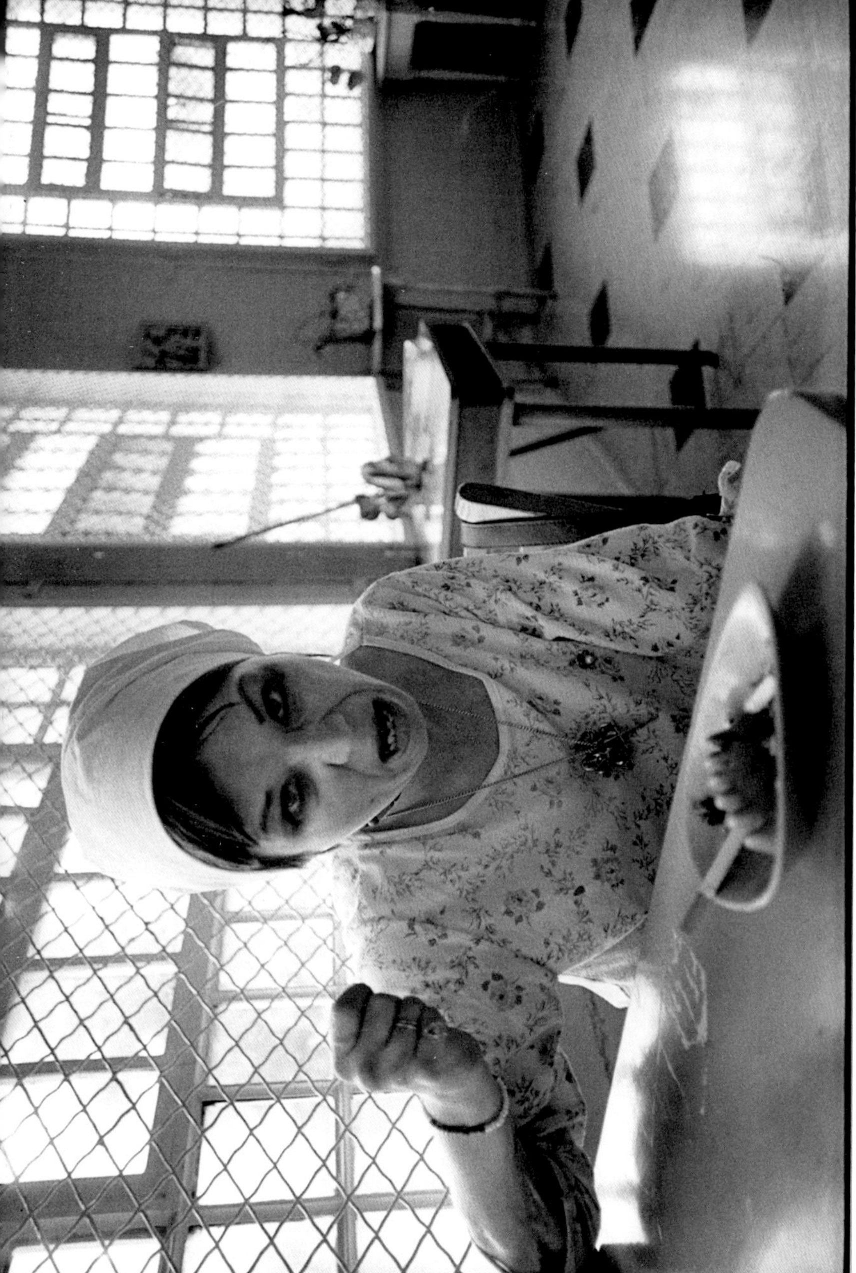

16. Leprosy patient with her nurse, National
Hansen's Disease Center. Carville, Louisiana, 1990.

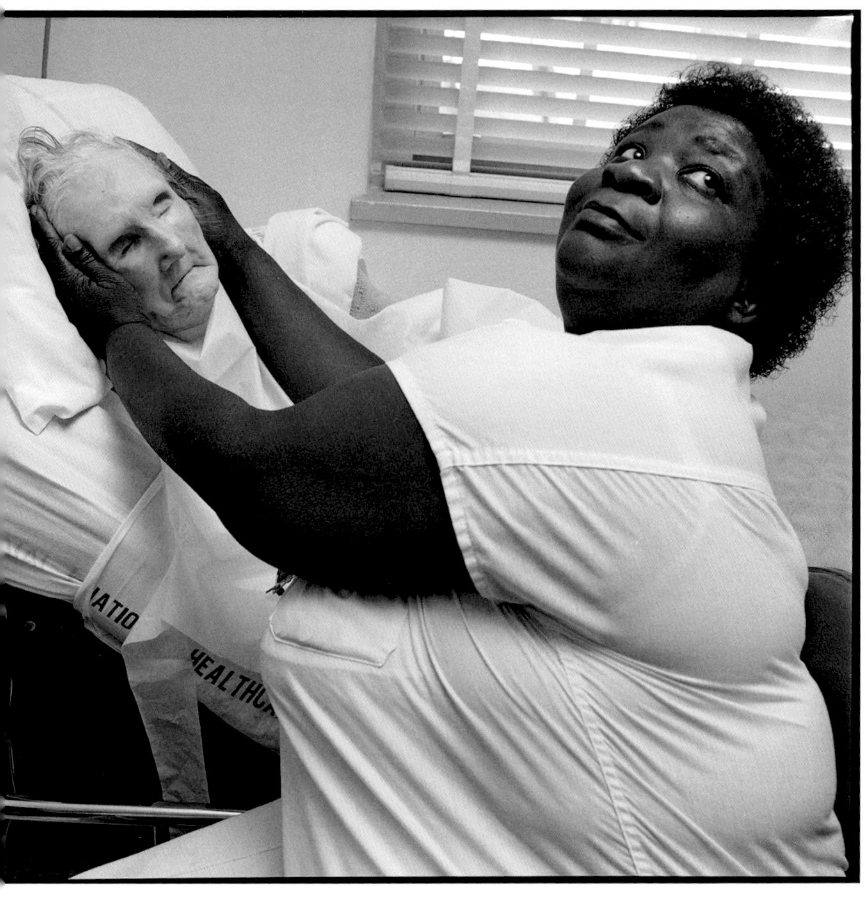

17. Feet in restraints, Ward 81, Oregon State Hospital.
Salem, Oregon, 1976.

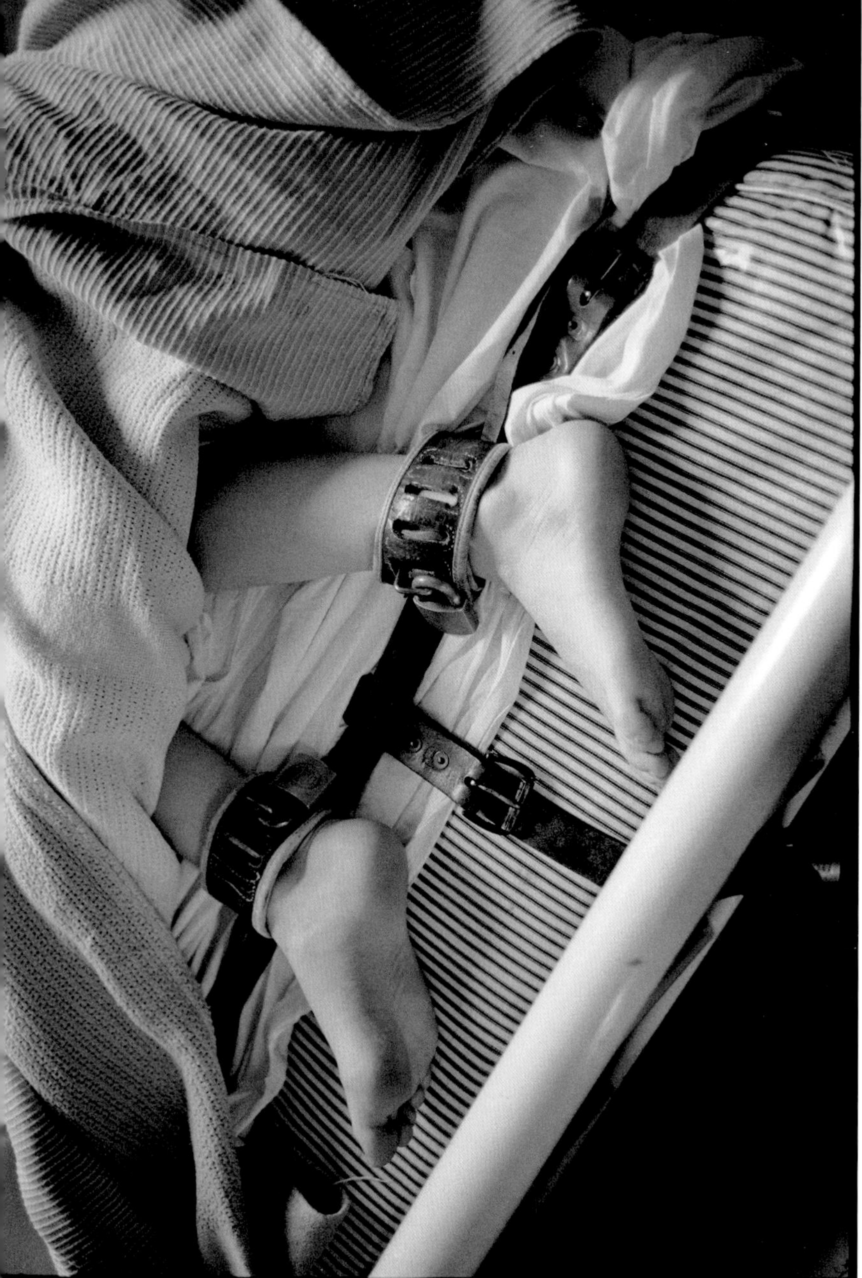

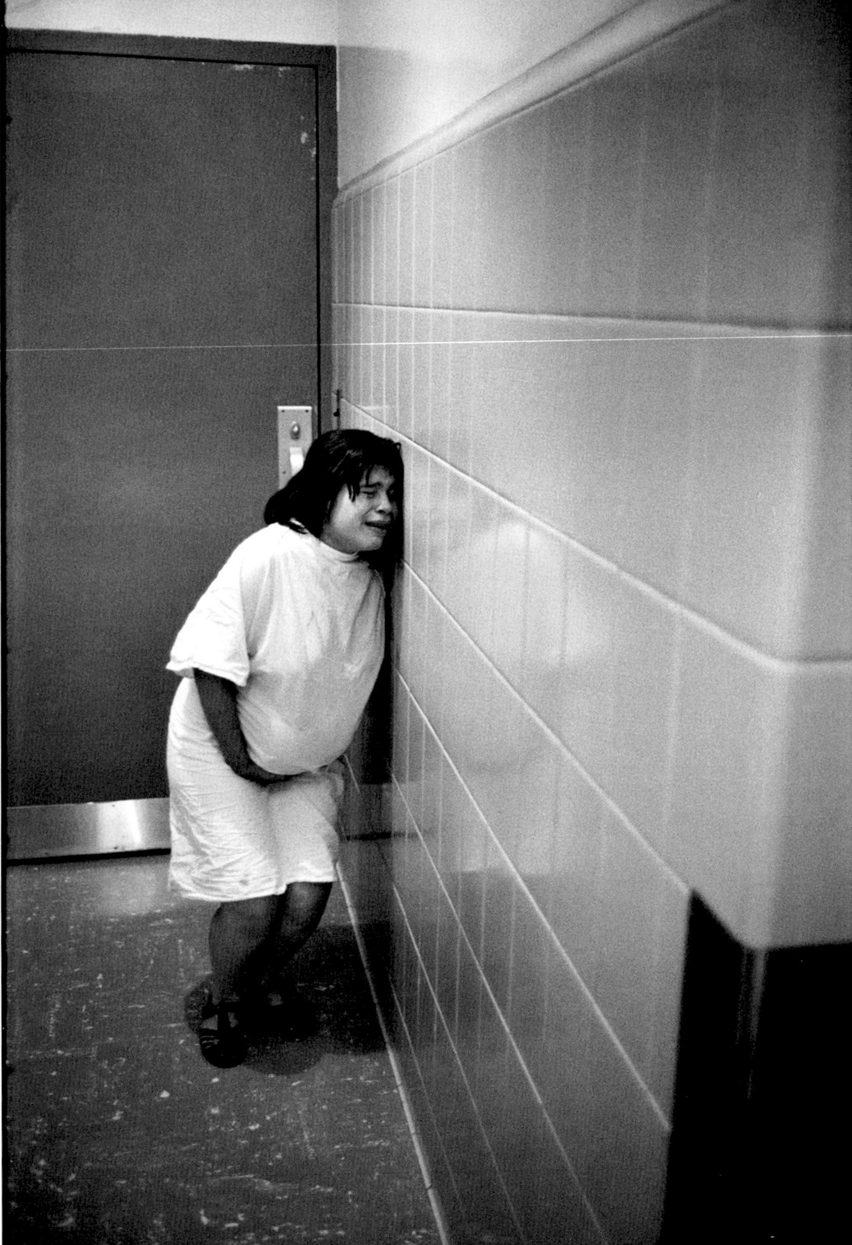

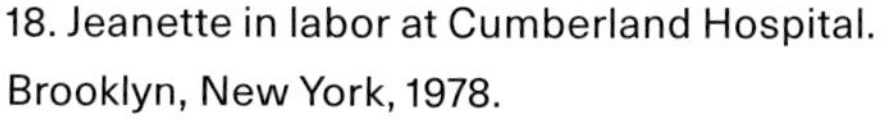

18. Jeanette in labor at Cumberland Hospital.
Brooklyn, New York, 1978.

19. Hydrocephalic girl and her sister,
Cottolengo hospital. Turin, Italy, 1990.

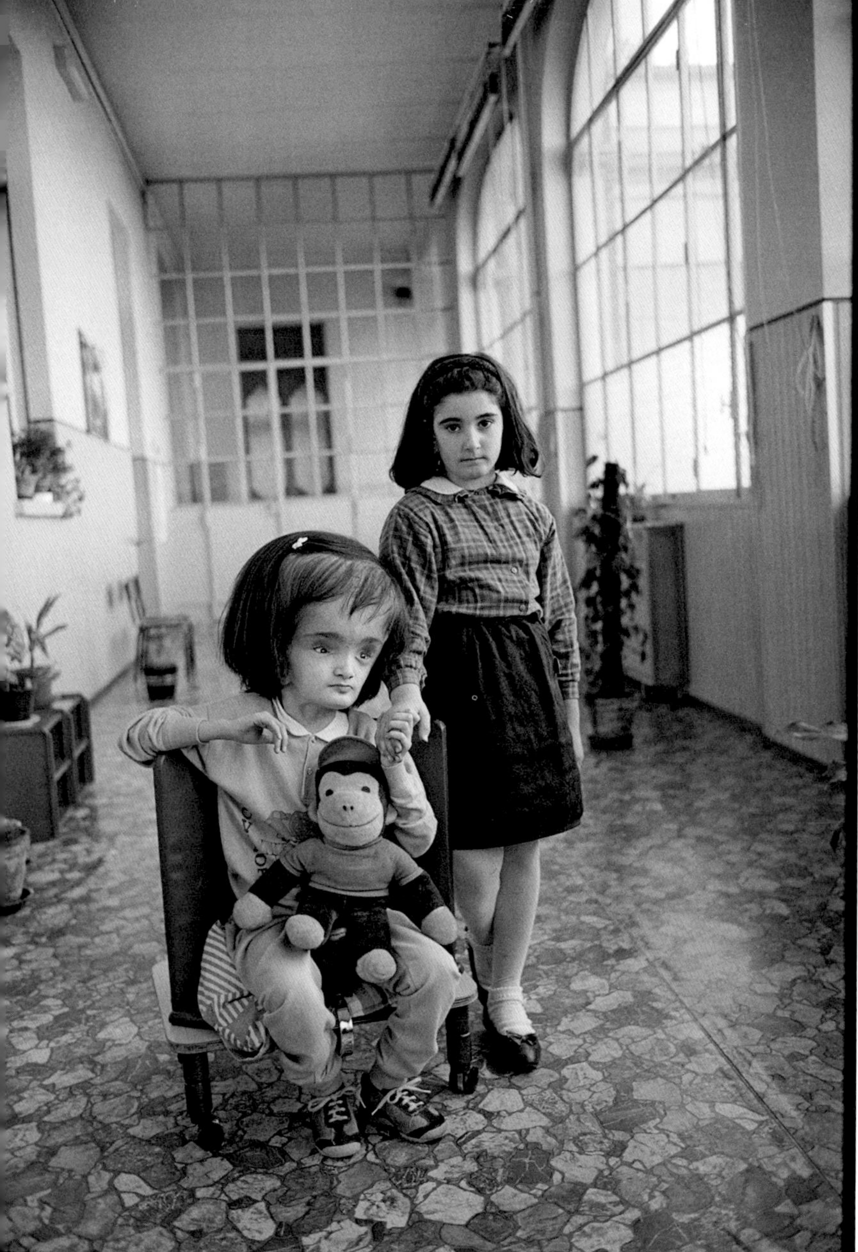

20. Keanna and LaShawndrea, Seattle, 1999.

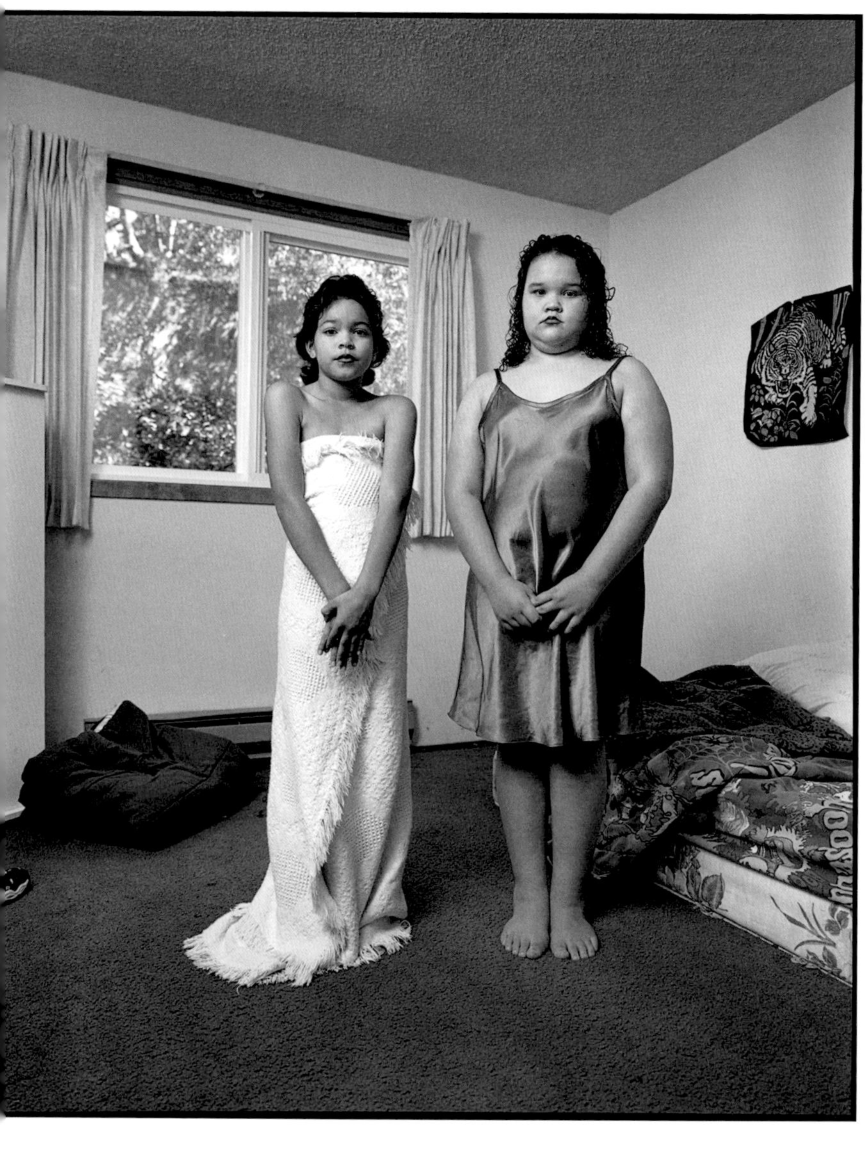

21. Mona with a photo of Michael Douglas, Ward 81,
Oregon State Hospital. Salem, Oregon, 1976.

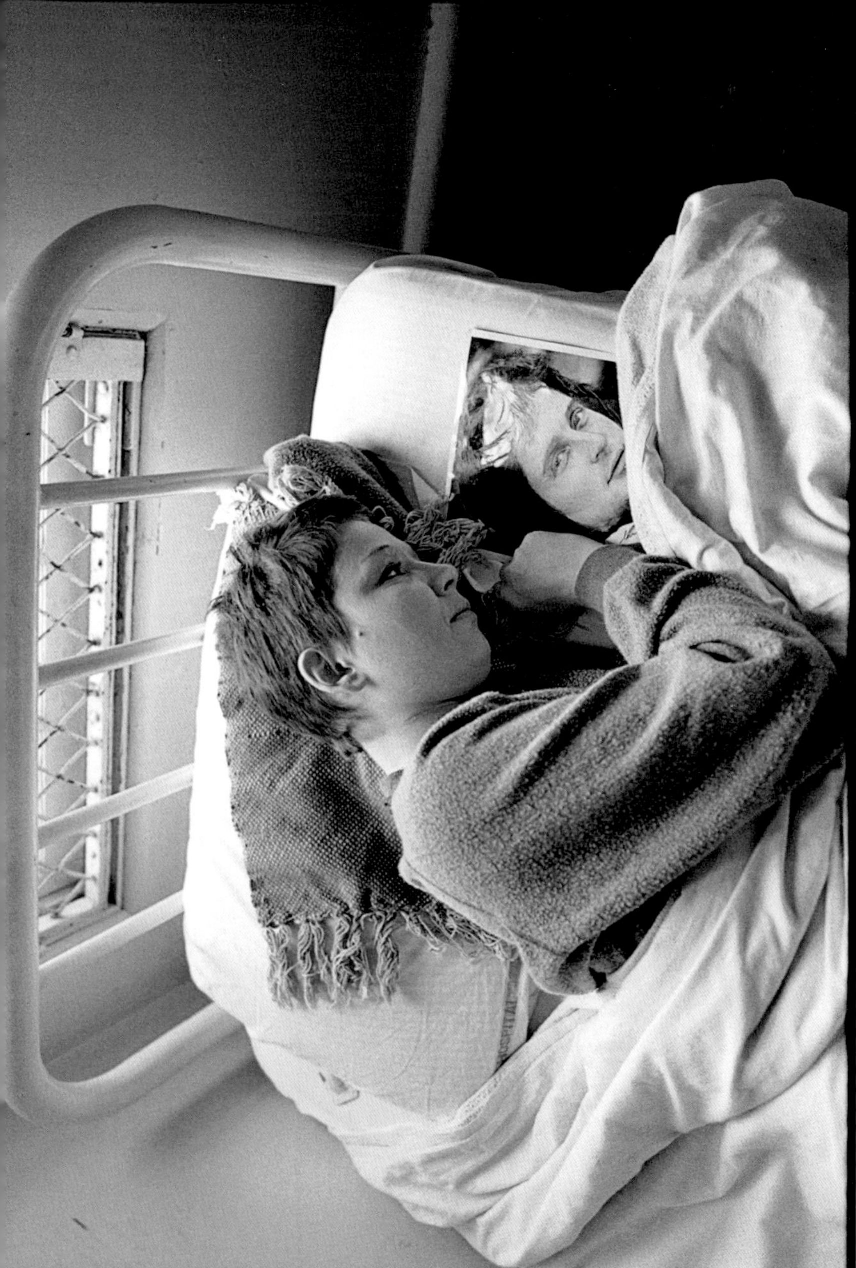

22. Heroin addict behind a door at
St. Clement's Drug Unit. London, 1969.

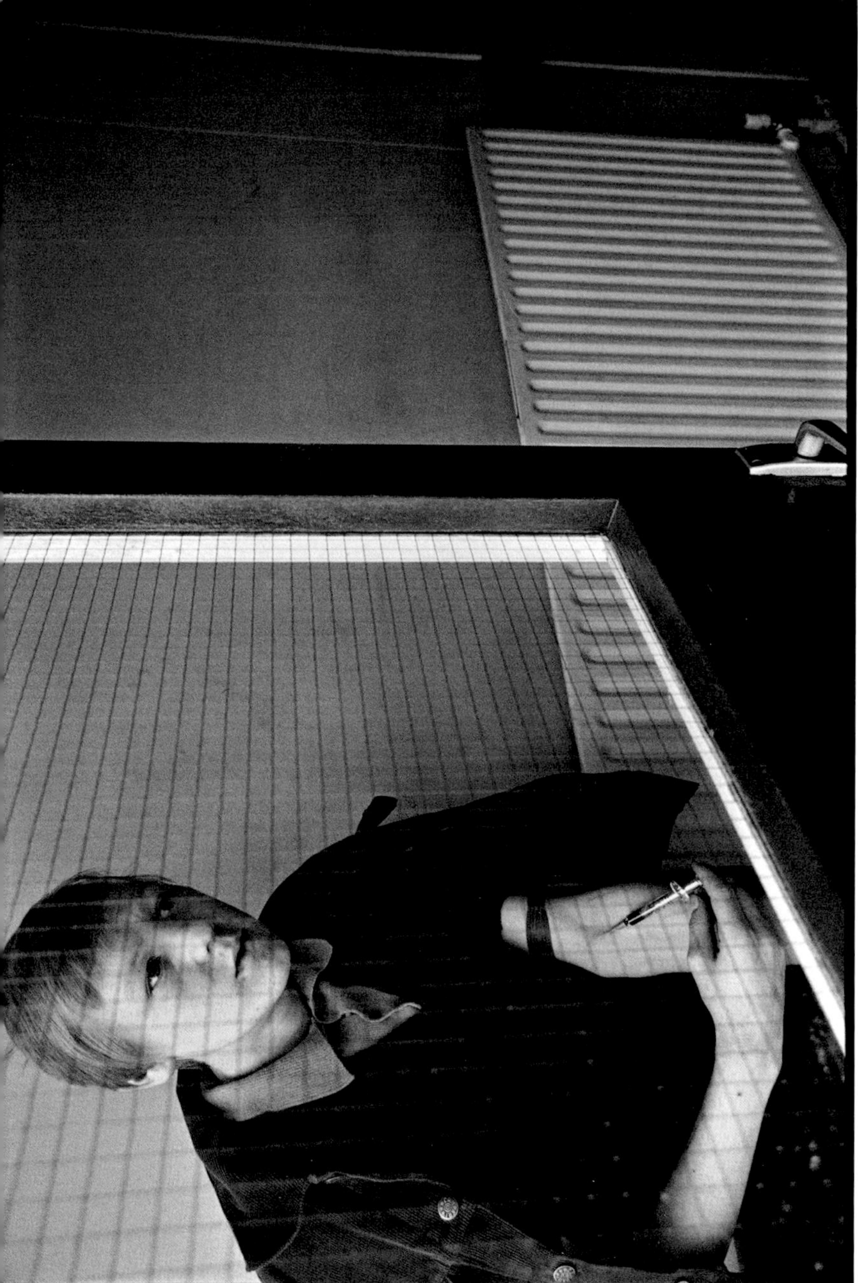

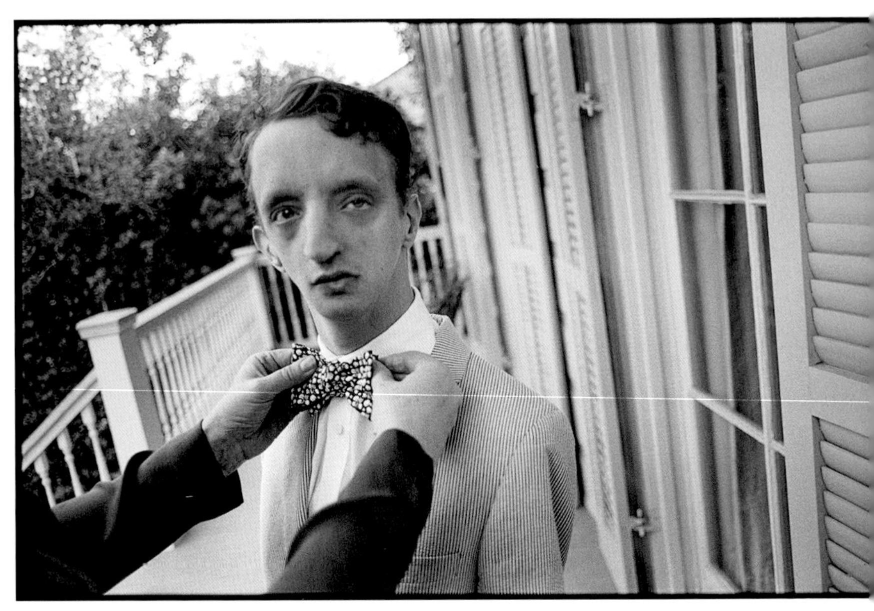

23. Thomas getting his bow tie fixed.
New Orleans, 2015.

24. Erin Blackwell, known as "Tiny,"
in juvenile detention. Seattle, 1983.

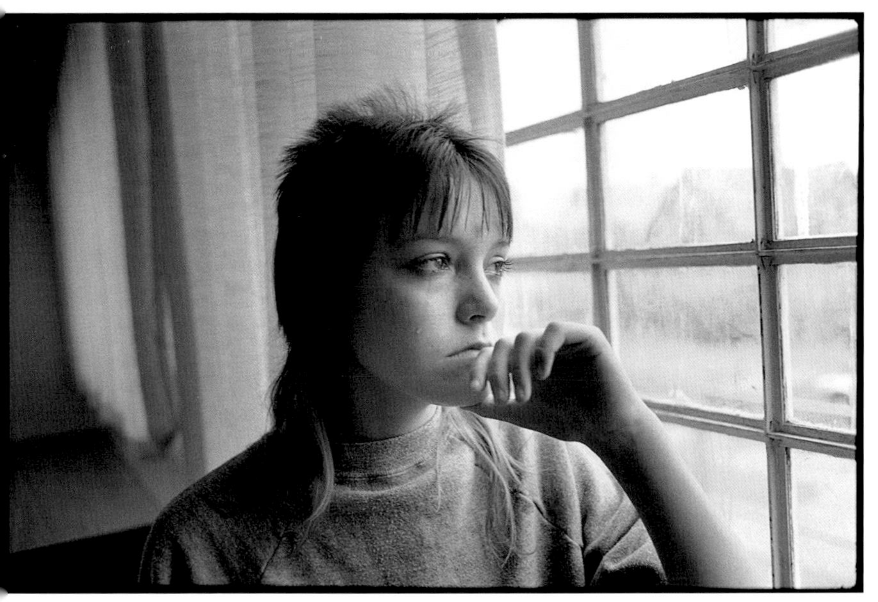

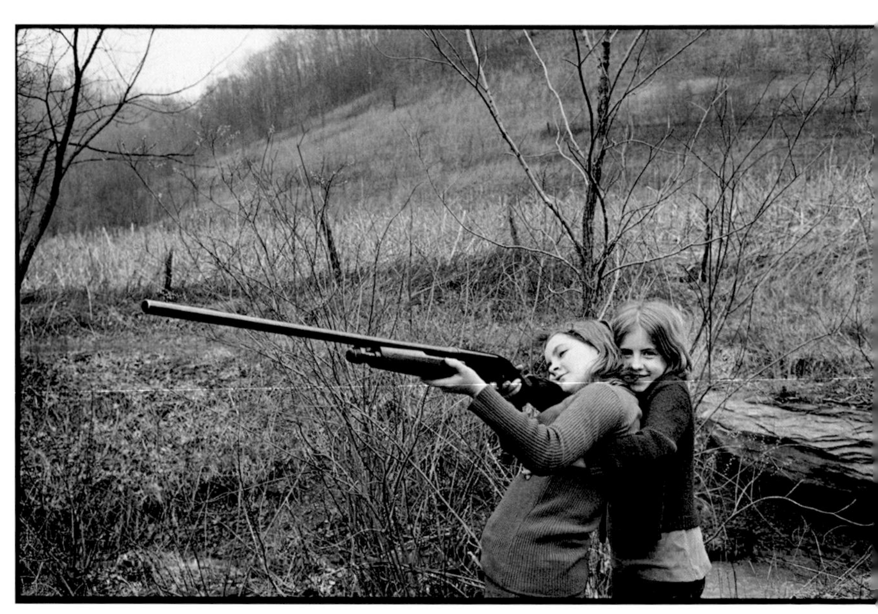

25. Girls playing with a gun. Harlan County, Kentucky, 1971.

26. Husband and wife, Harlan County, Kentucky, 1971.

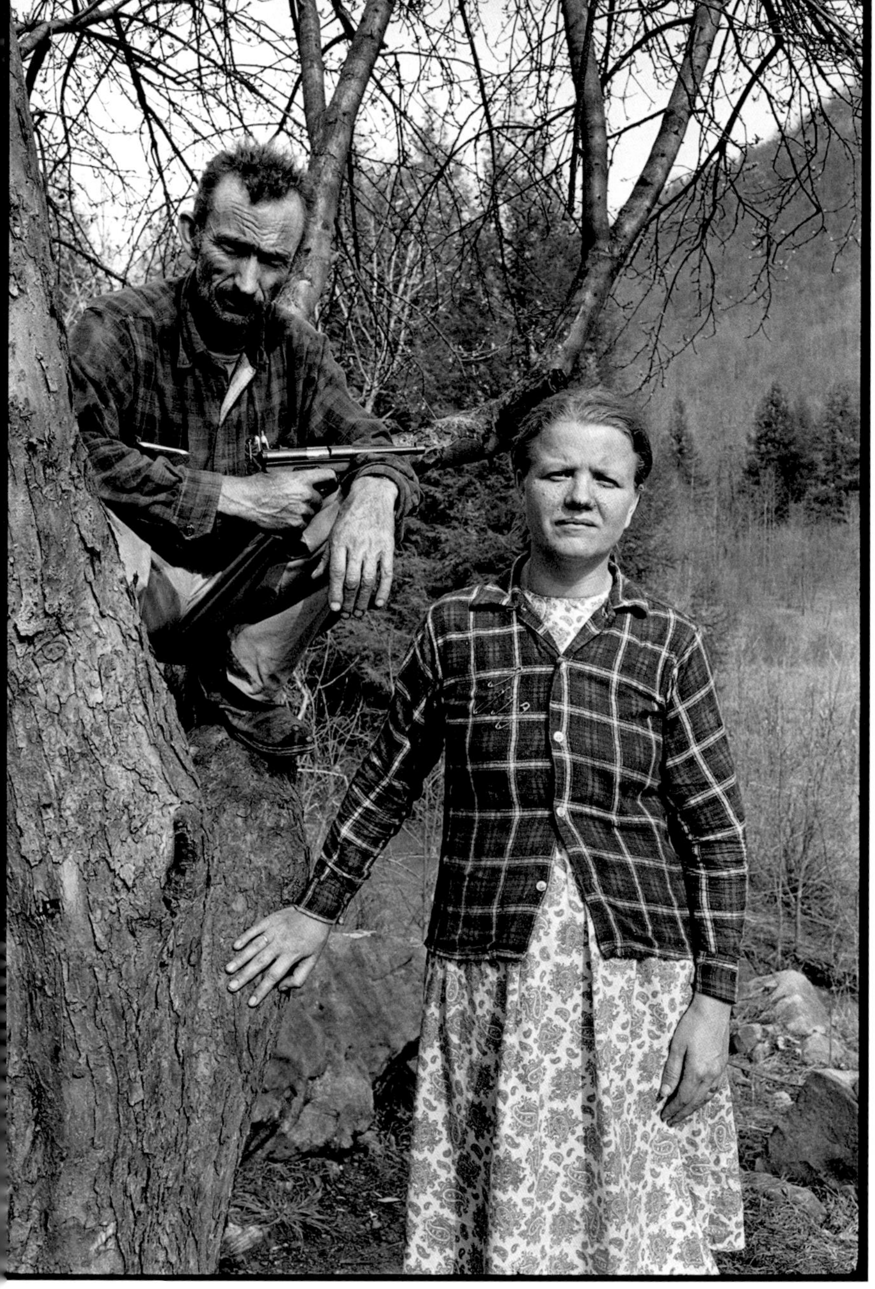

27. Tiny in her Halloween costume. Seattle, 1983.

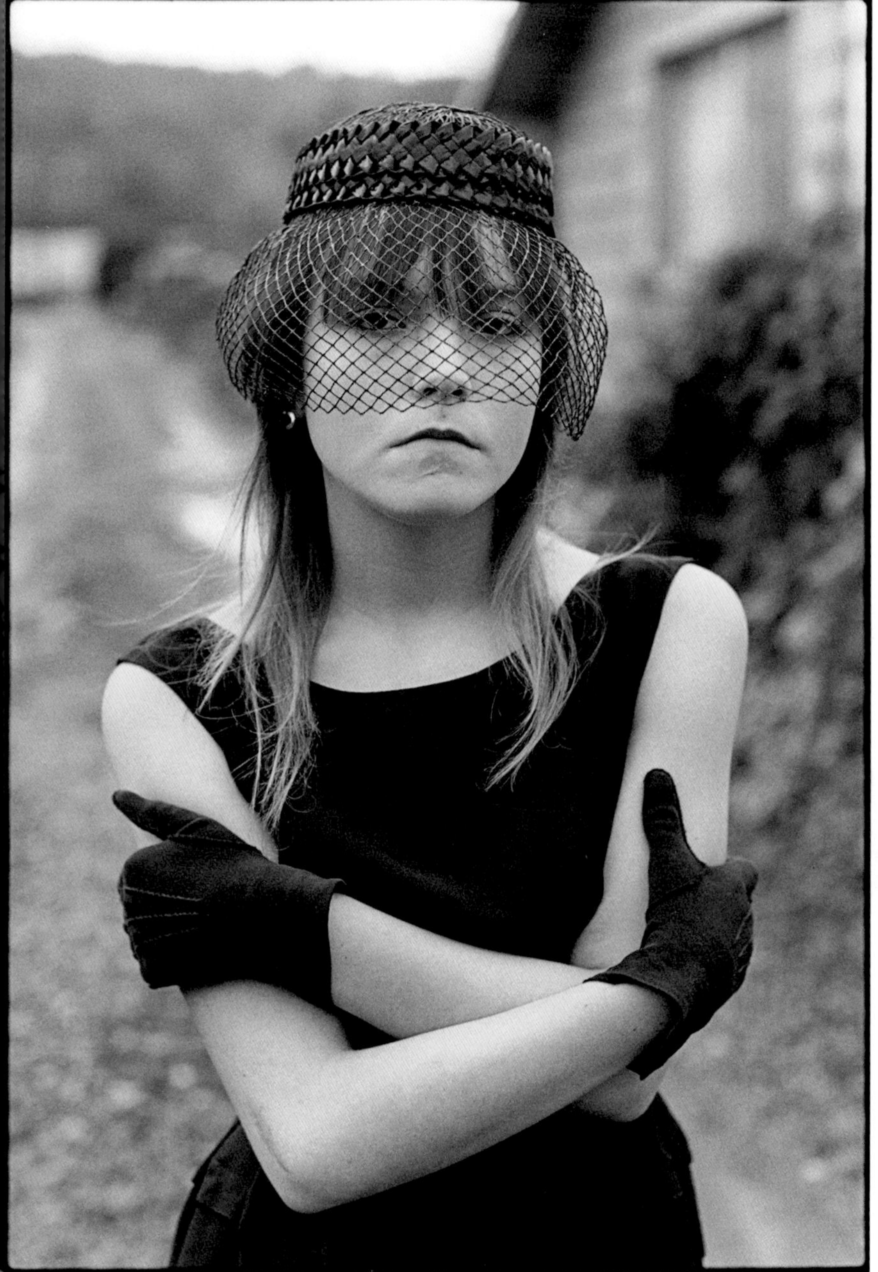

28. Tiny standing on Pike Street. Seattle, 1983.

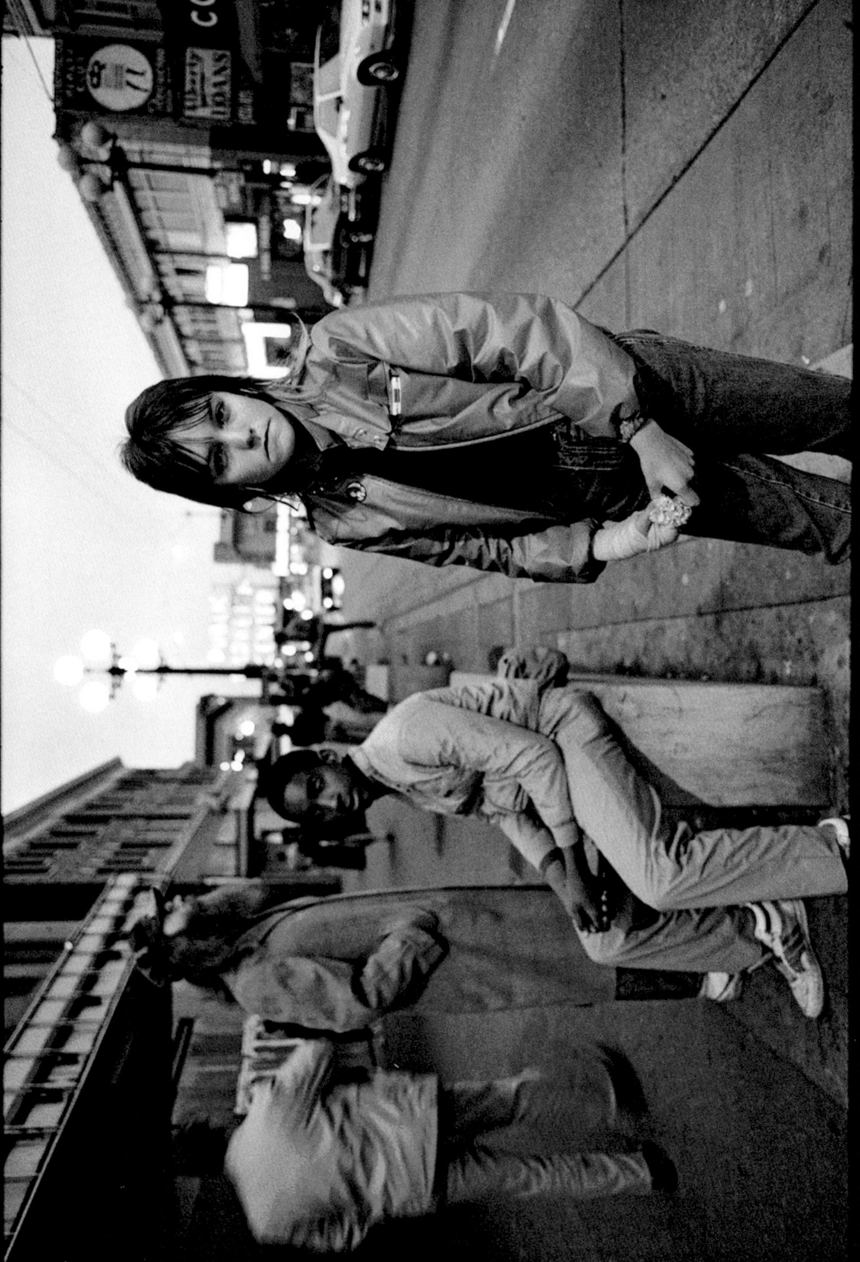

29. Amanda and her cousin Amy.
Valdese, North Carolina, 1990.

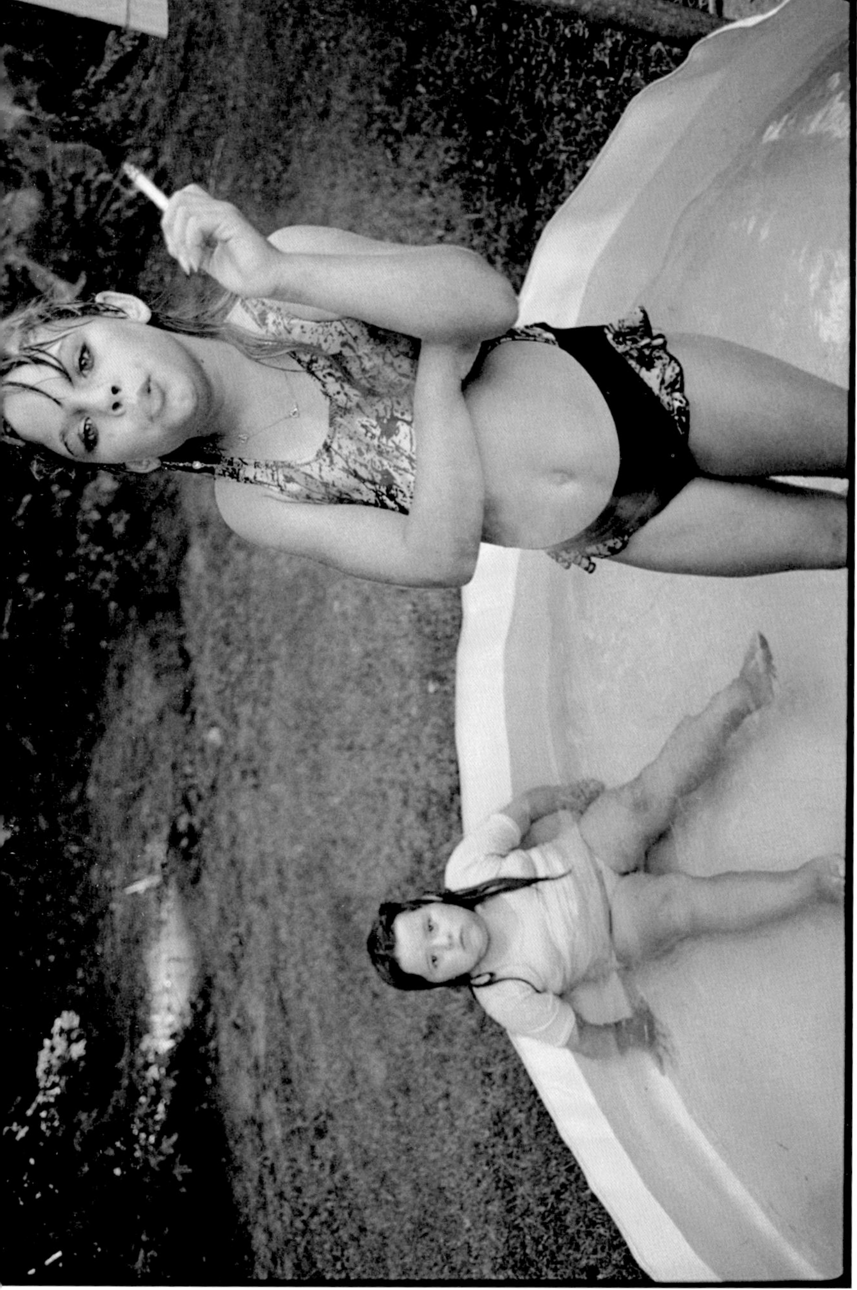

30. "Rat" and Mike with a gun. Seattle, 1983.

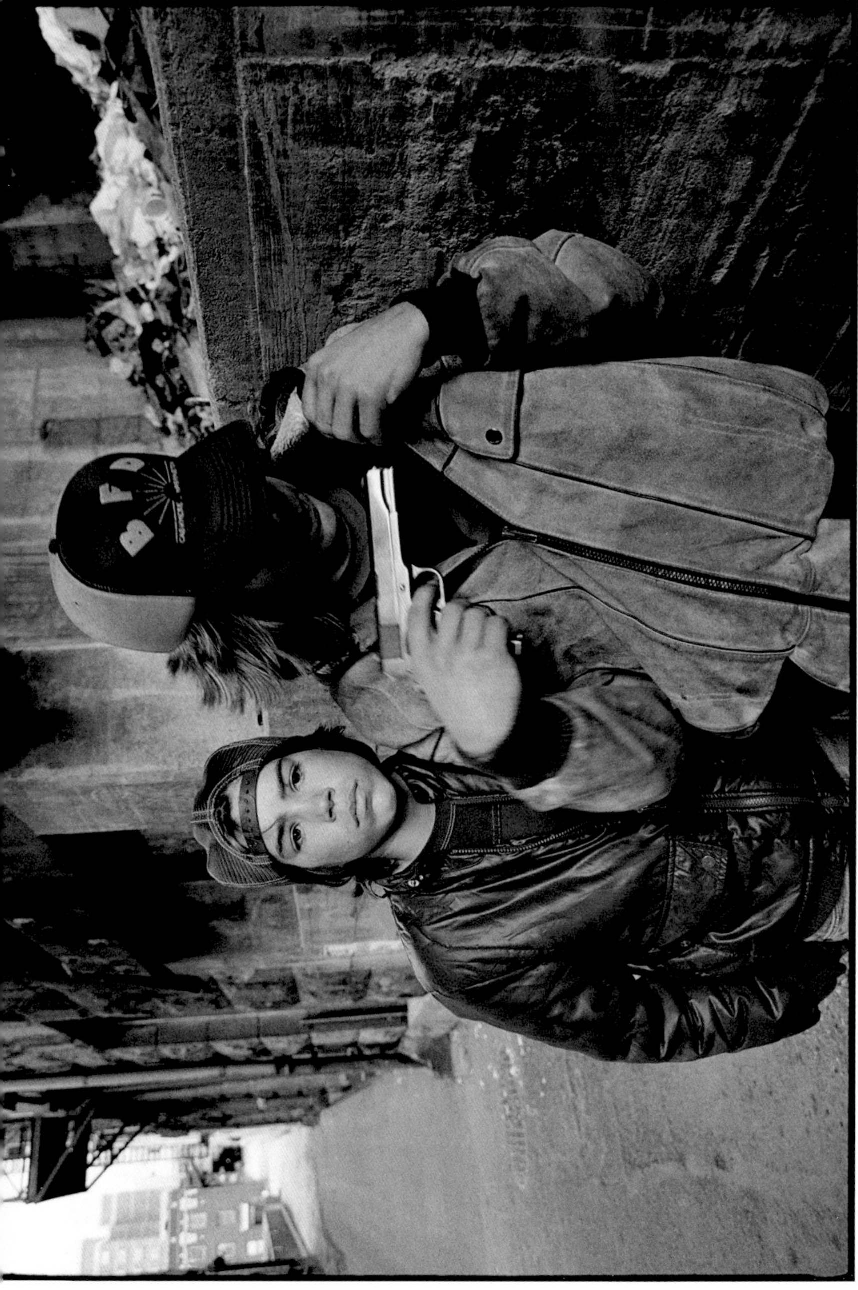

31. Pike Street, Seattle, 1983.

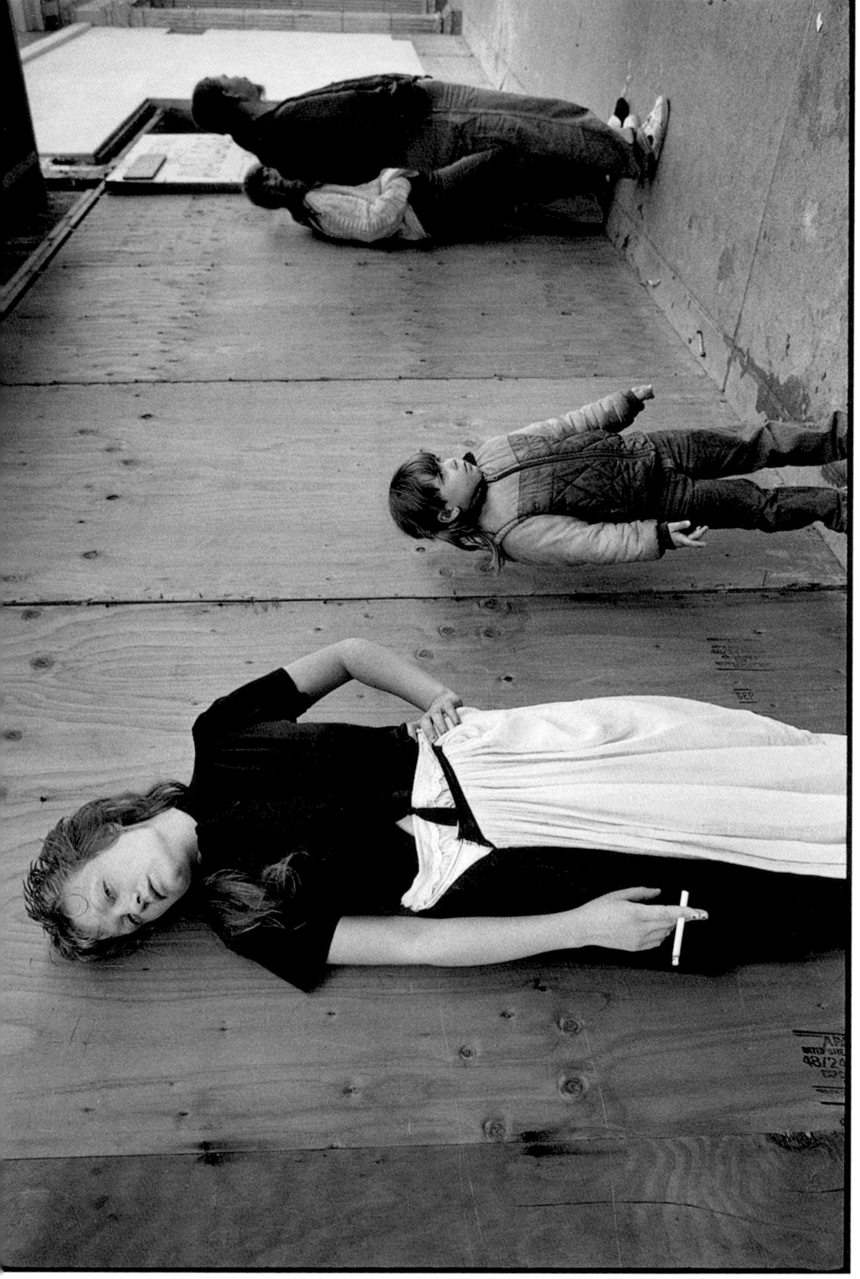

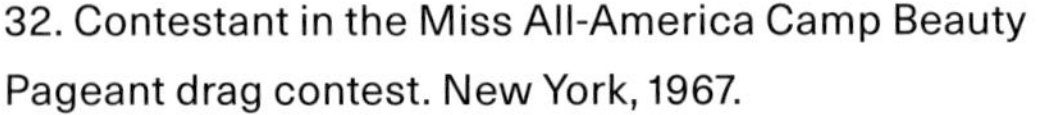

32. Contestant in the Miss All-America Camp Beauty
Pageant drag contest. New York, 1967.

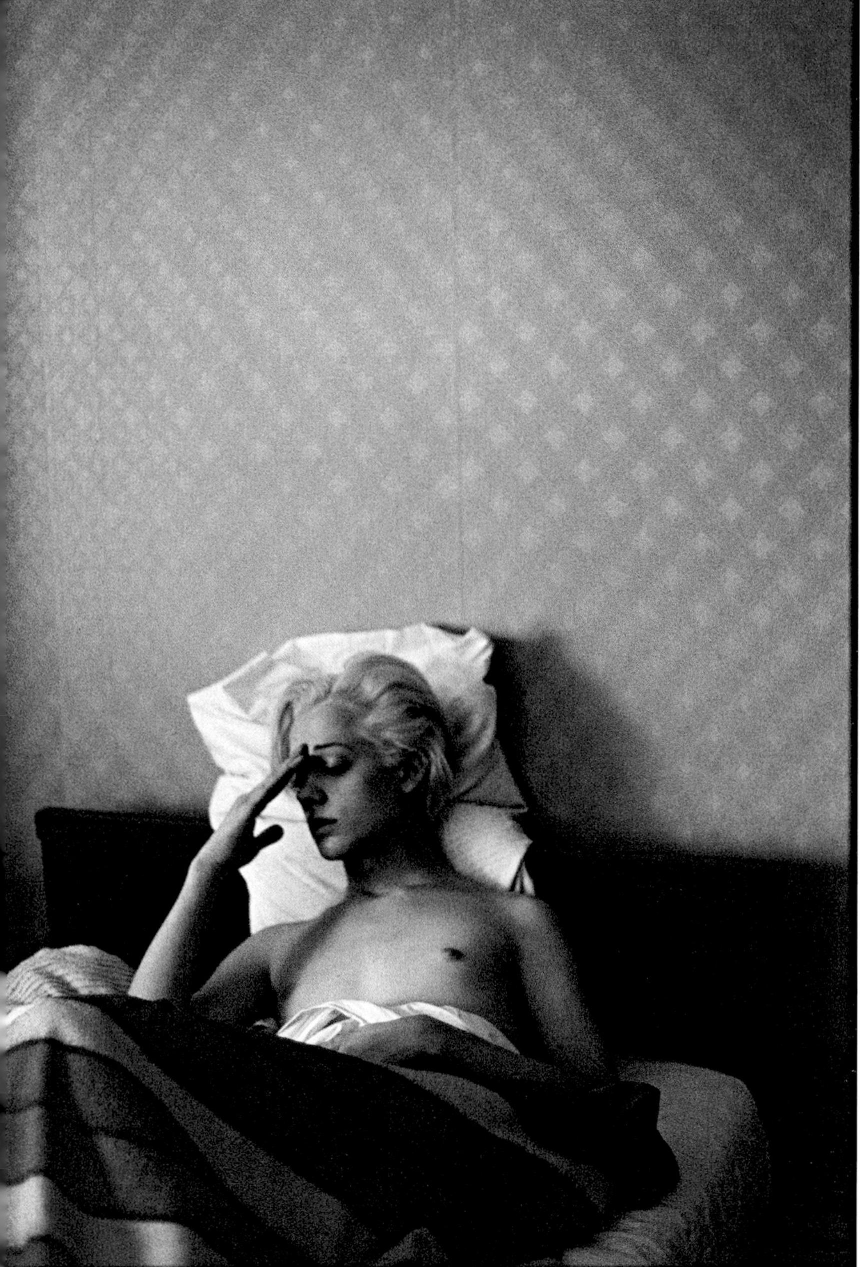

33. Erin pregnant with Daylon, Seattle, 1985.

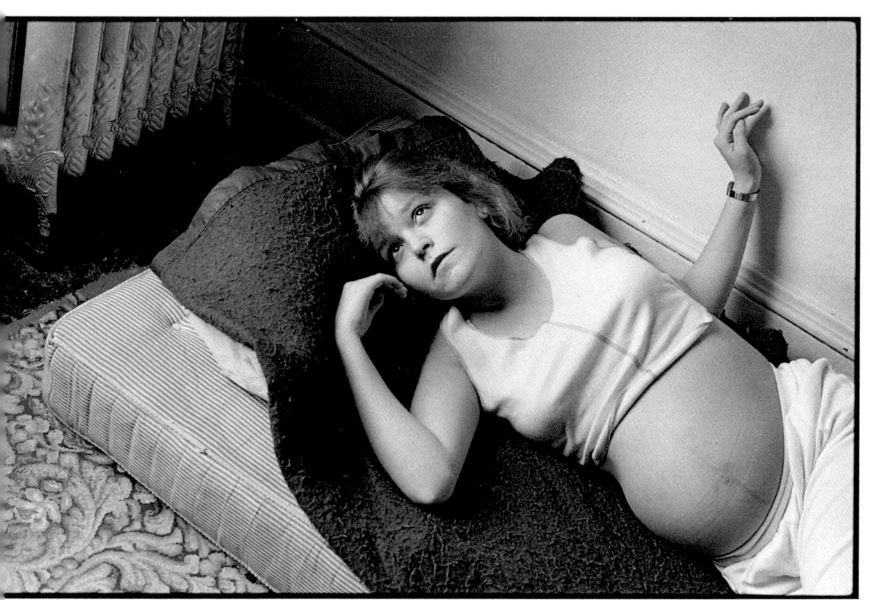

34. Breann Benedict at a government emergency
housing site. Grand Forks, North Dakota, 1997.

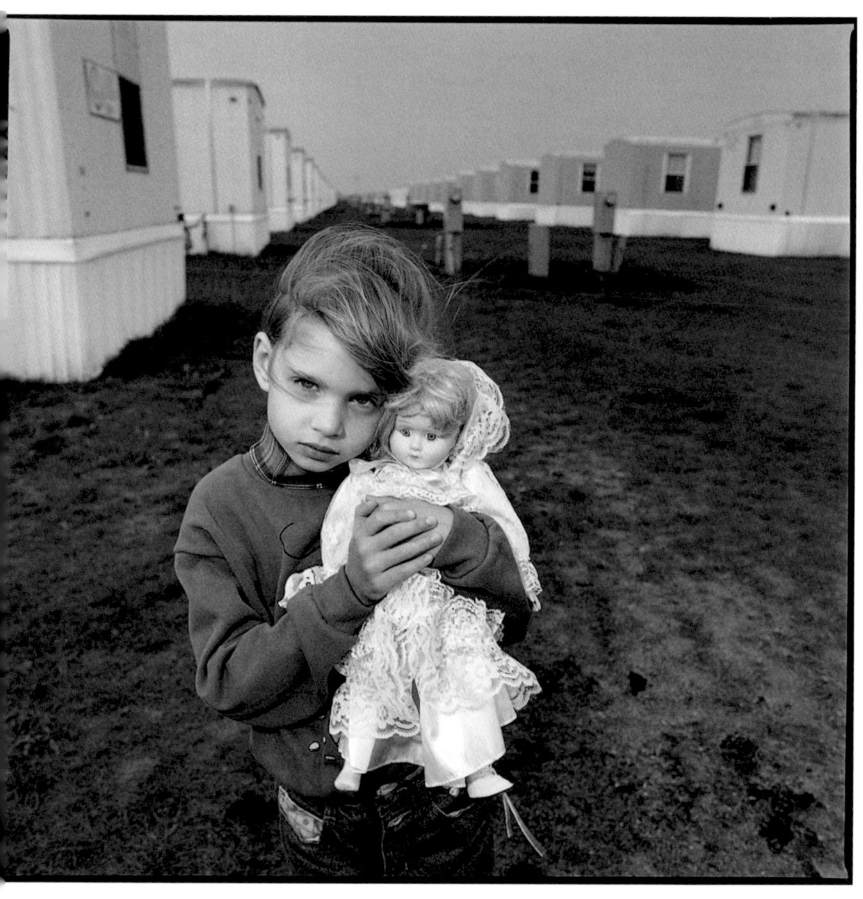

35. Crissy, Jesse, Linda, and Dean Damm in their car.
Los Angeles, 1987.

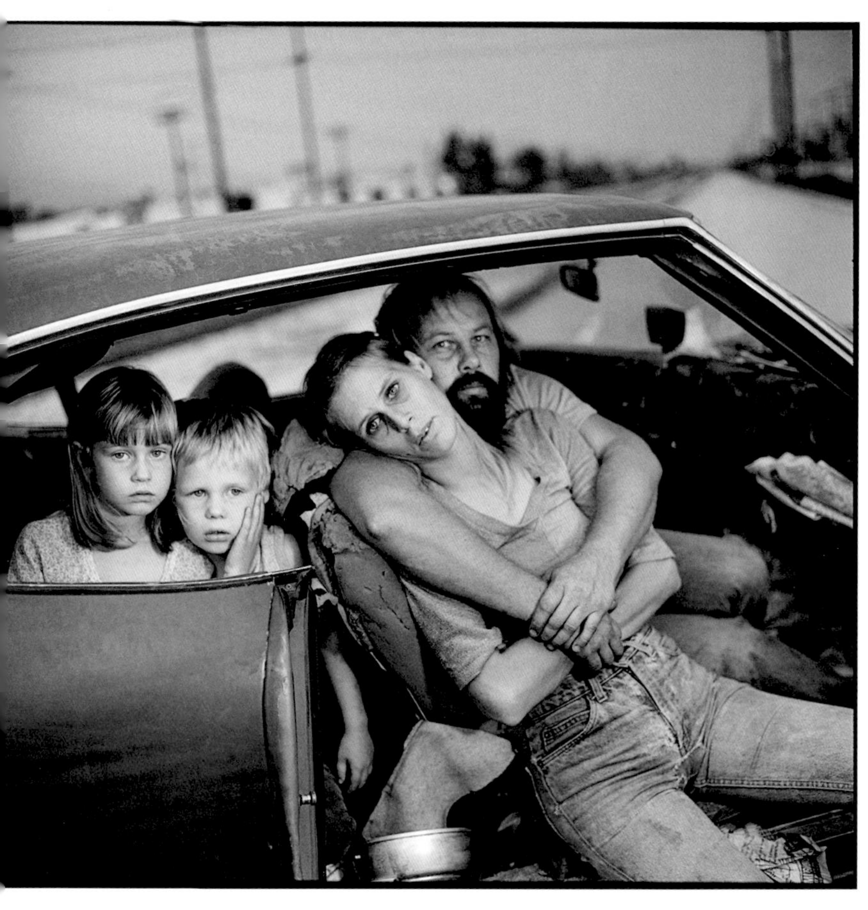

36. Crissy, Dean, and Linda. Llano, California, 1994.

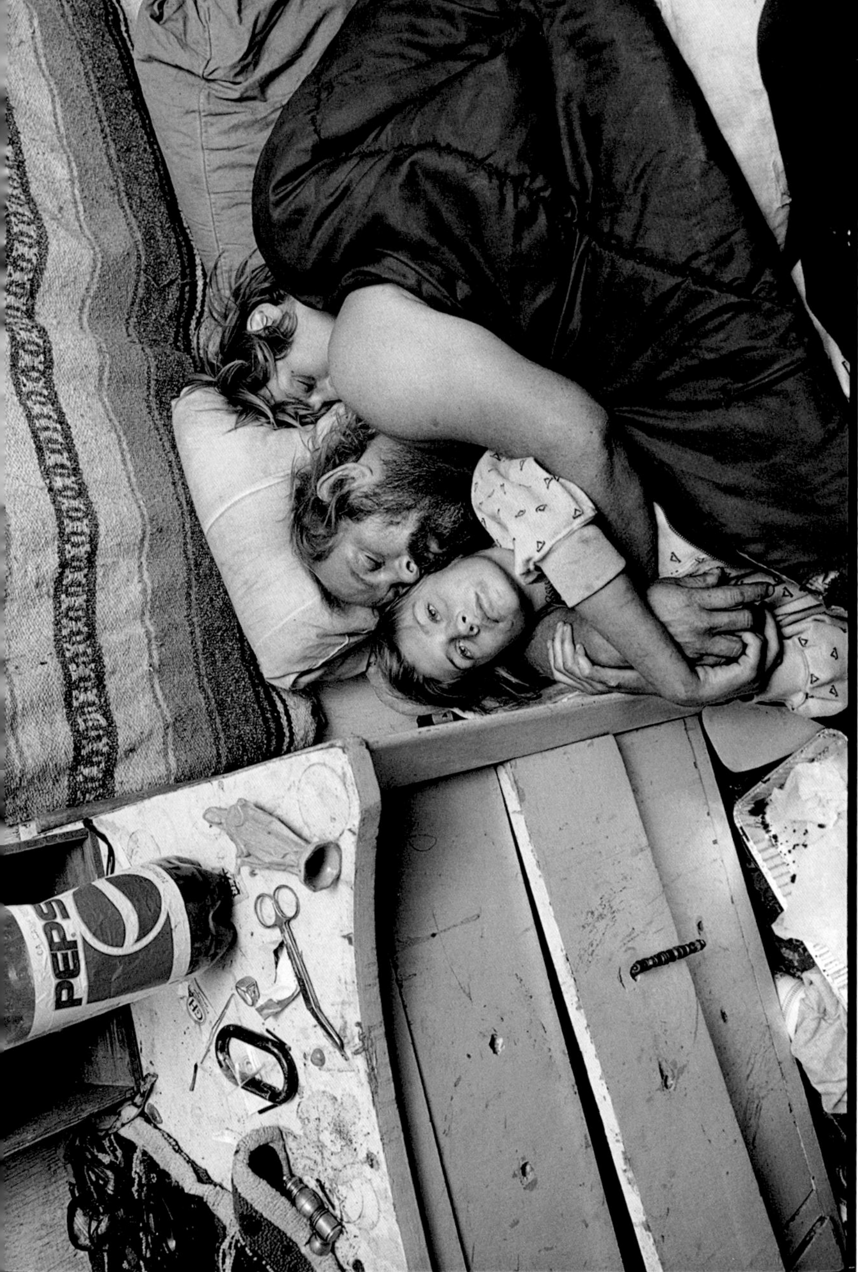

37. Crissy and her boyfriend, Adam. Llano, California, 1994.

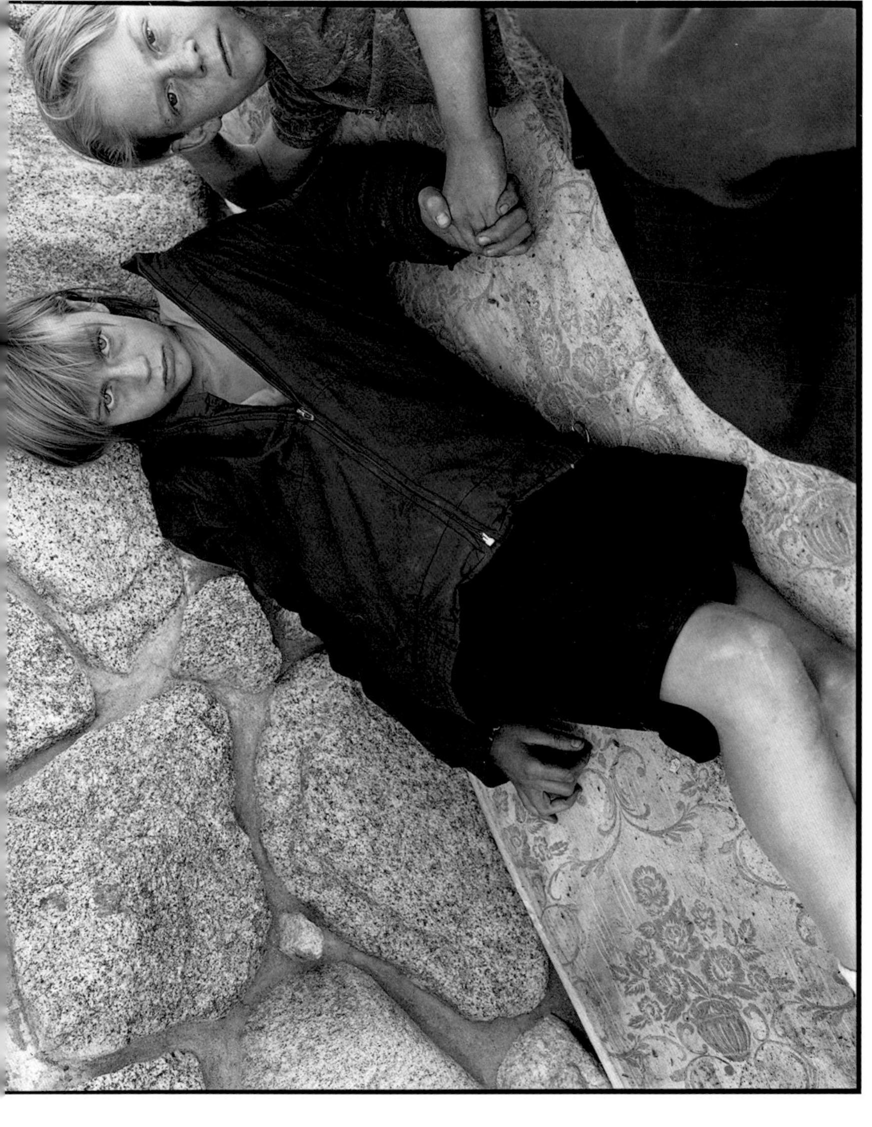

38. Putla in front of a mirror.
Falkland Road, Mumbai, 1978.

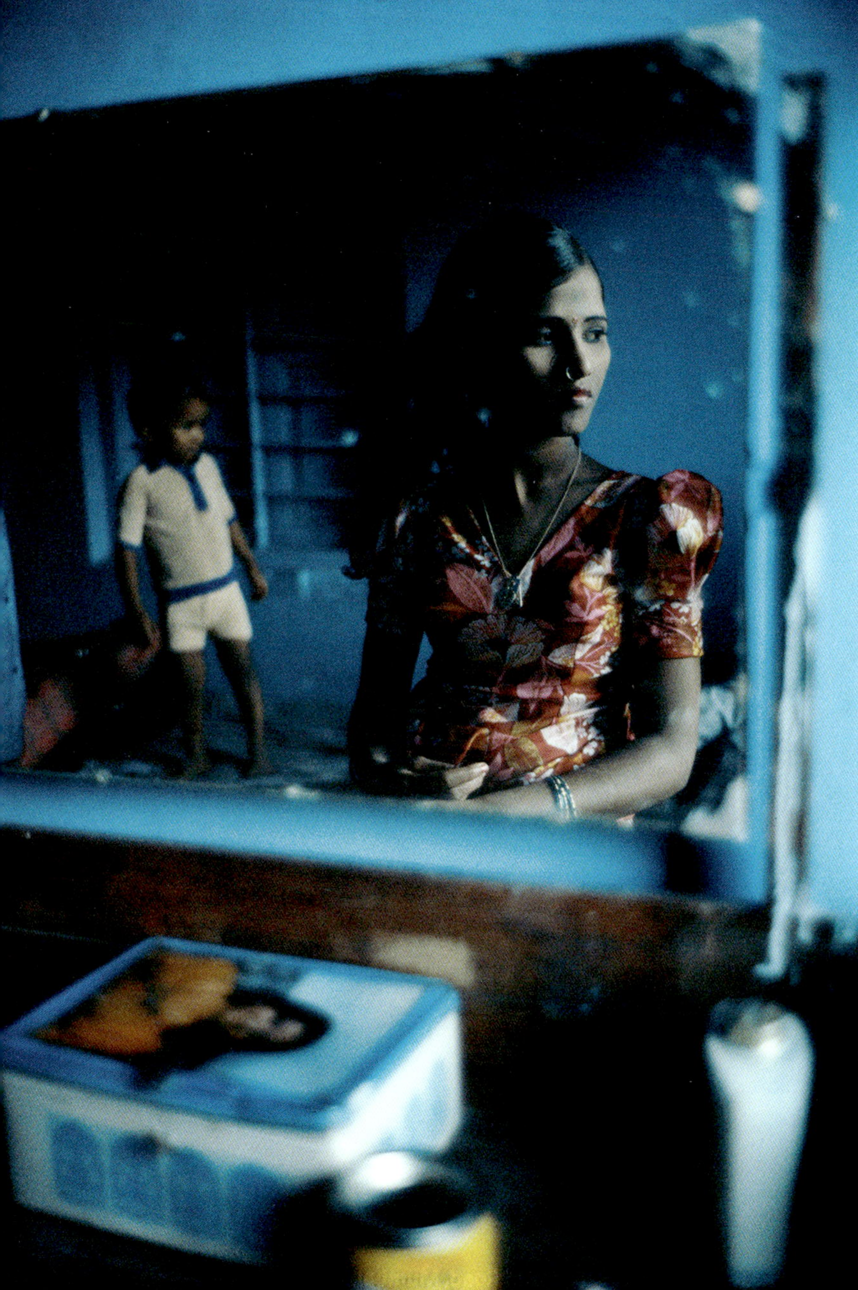

39. Lata lying in bed. Falkland Road, Mumbai, 1978.

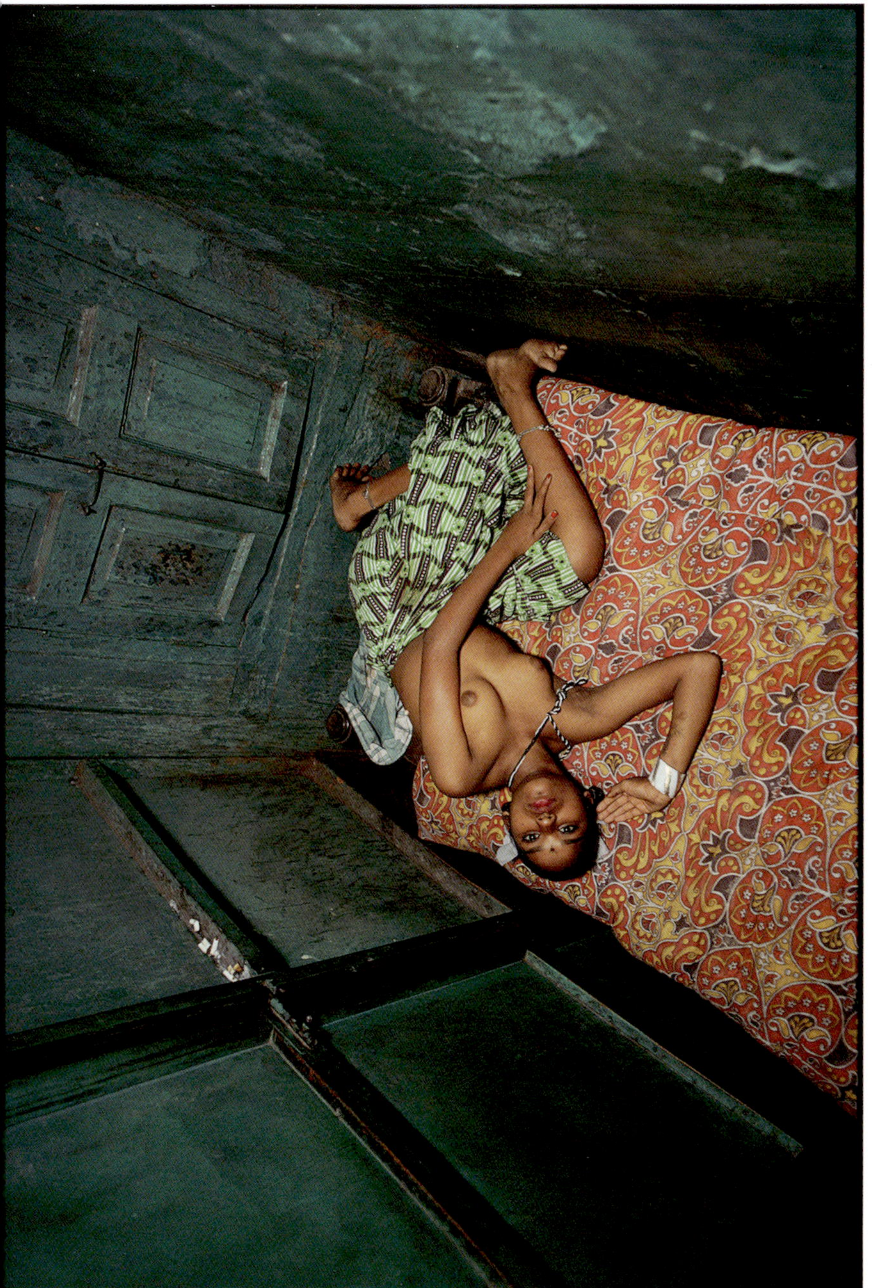

40. Falkland Road, Mumbai, 1978.

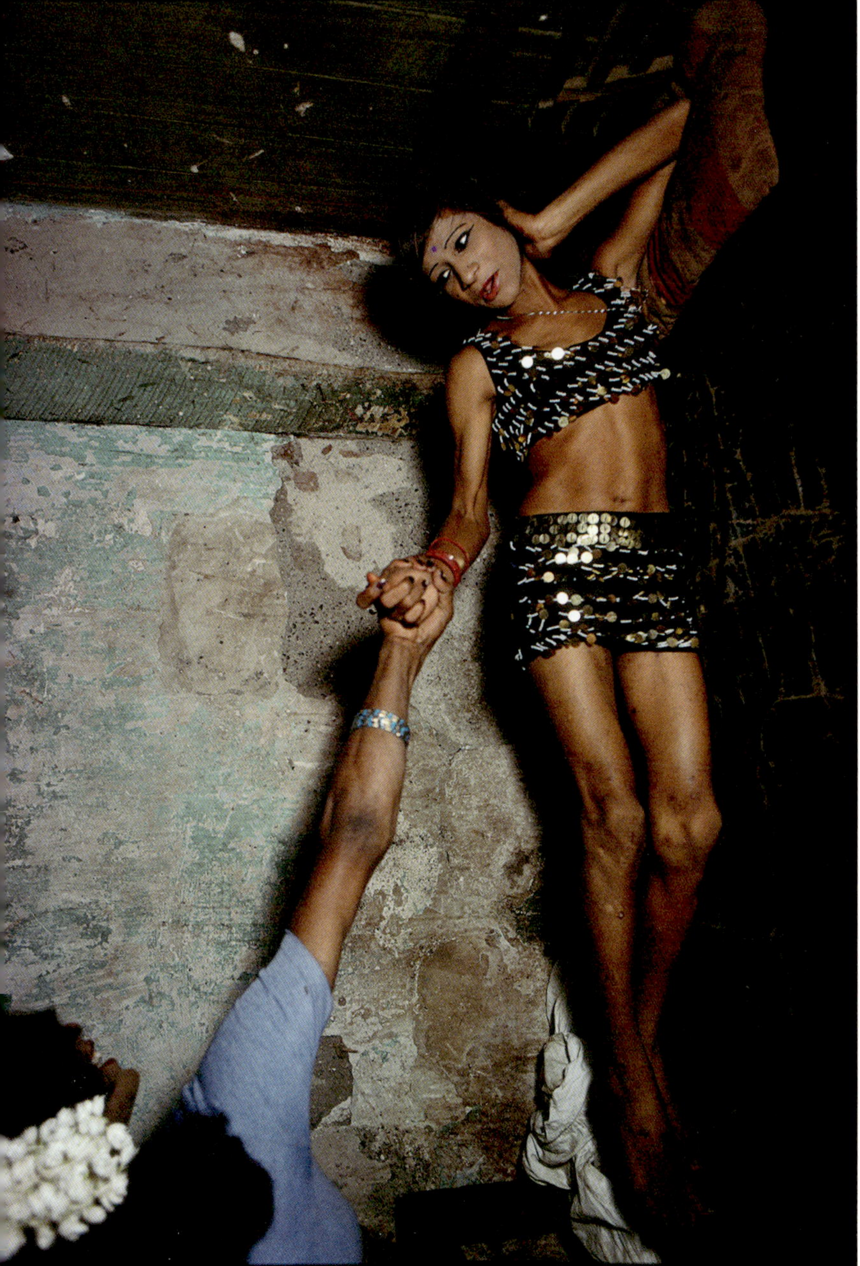

41. Putting on lipstick. Falkland Road, Mumbai, 1978.

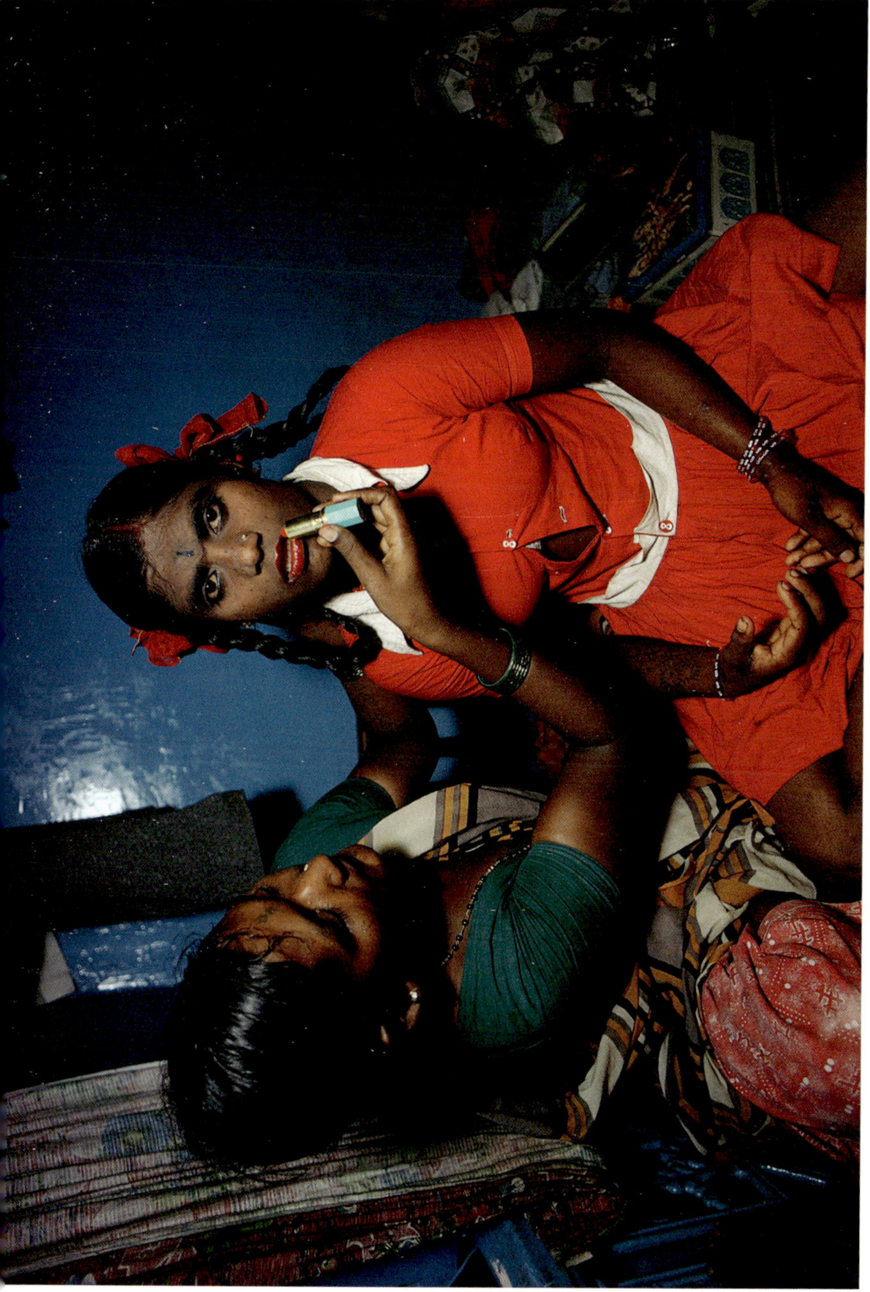

42. Erin fighting with her mother, Pat. Seattle, 1999.

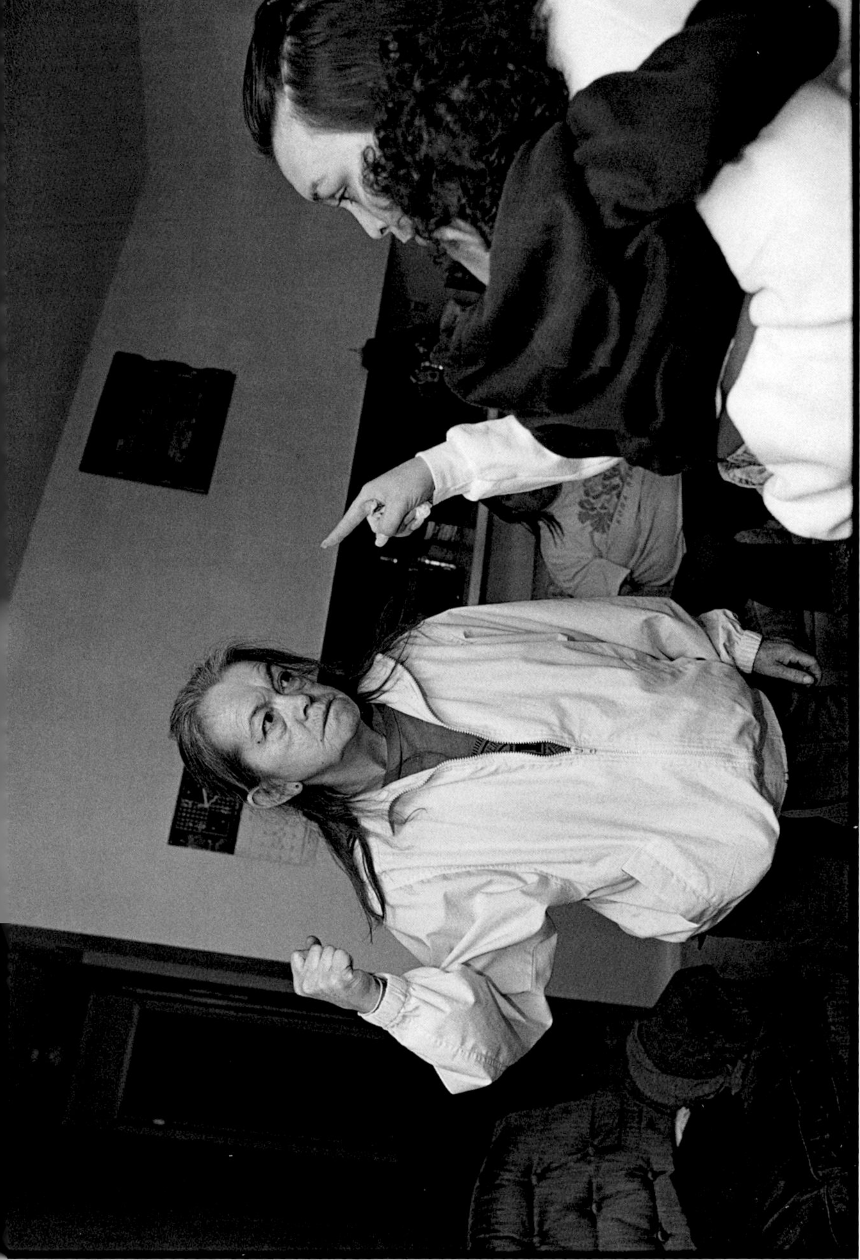

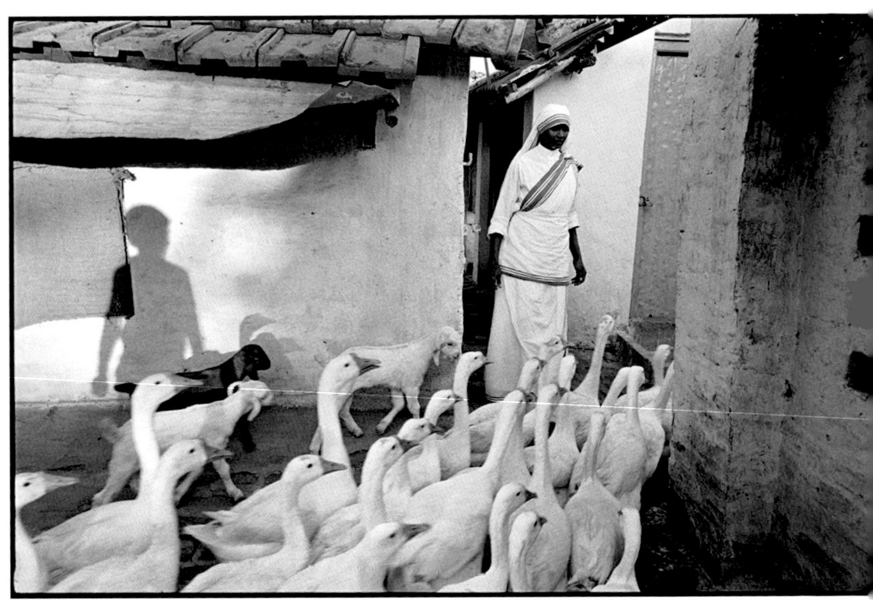

43. Shanti Nagar Leprosy Hospital,
near Asansol, India, 1981.

44. Mother Teresa feeding a man at the Home
for the Dying, Mother Teresa's Missionaries
of Charity. Kolkata, India, 1980.

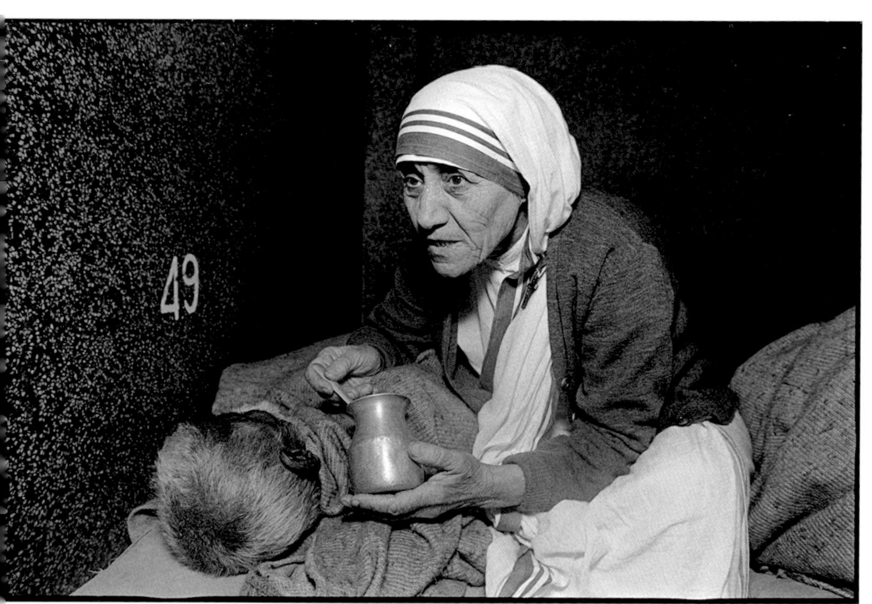
49

45. James and Natasha Gurley.
Valdese, North Carolina, 1990.

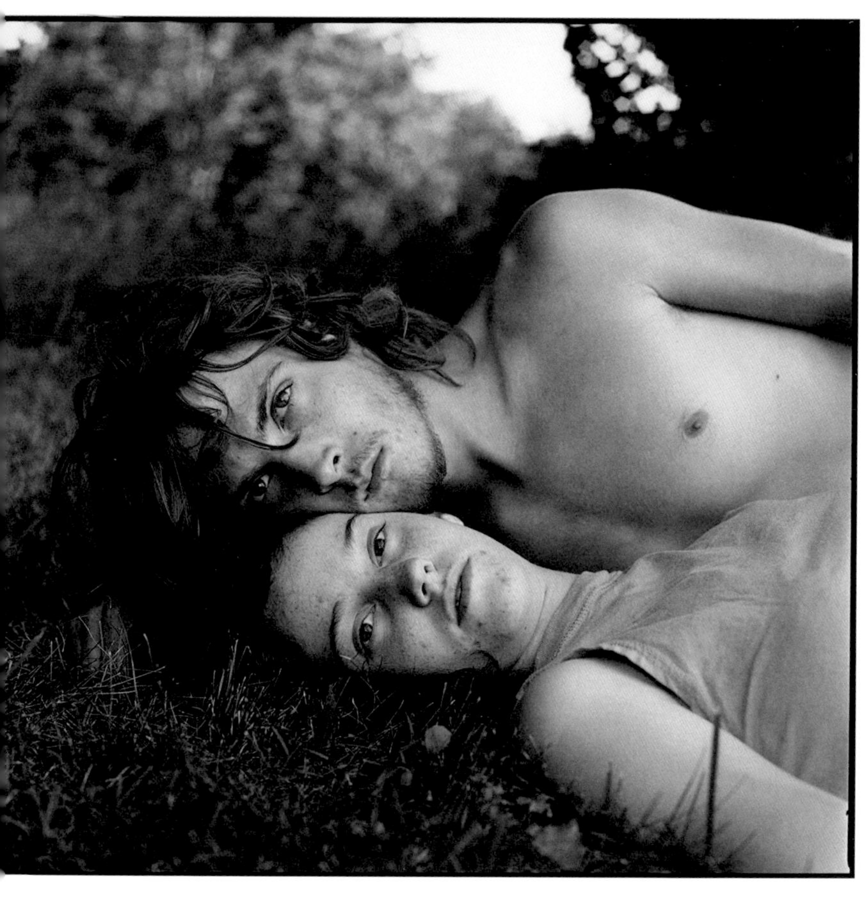

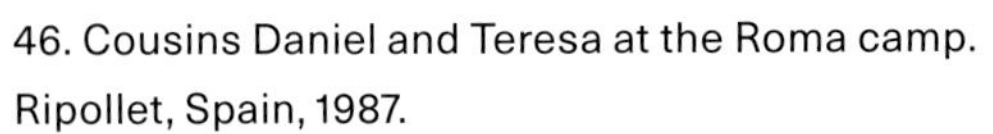

46. Cousins Daniel and Teresa at the Roma camp.
Ripollet, Spain, 1987.

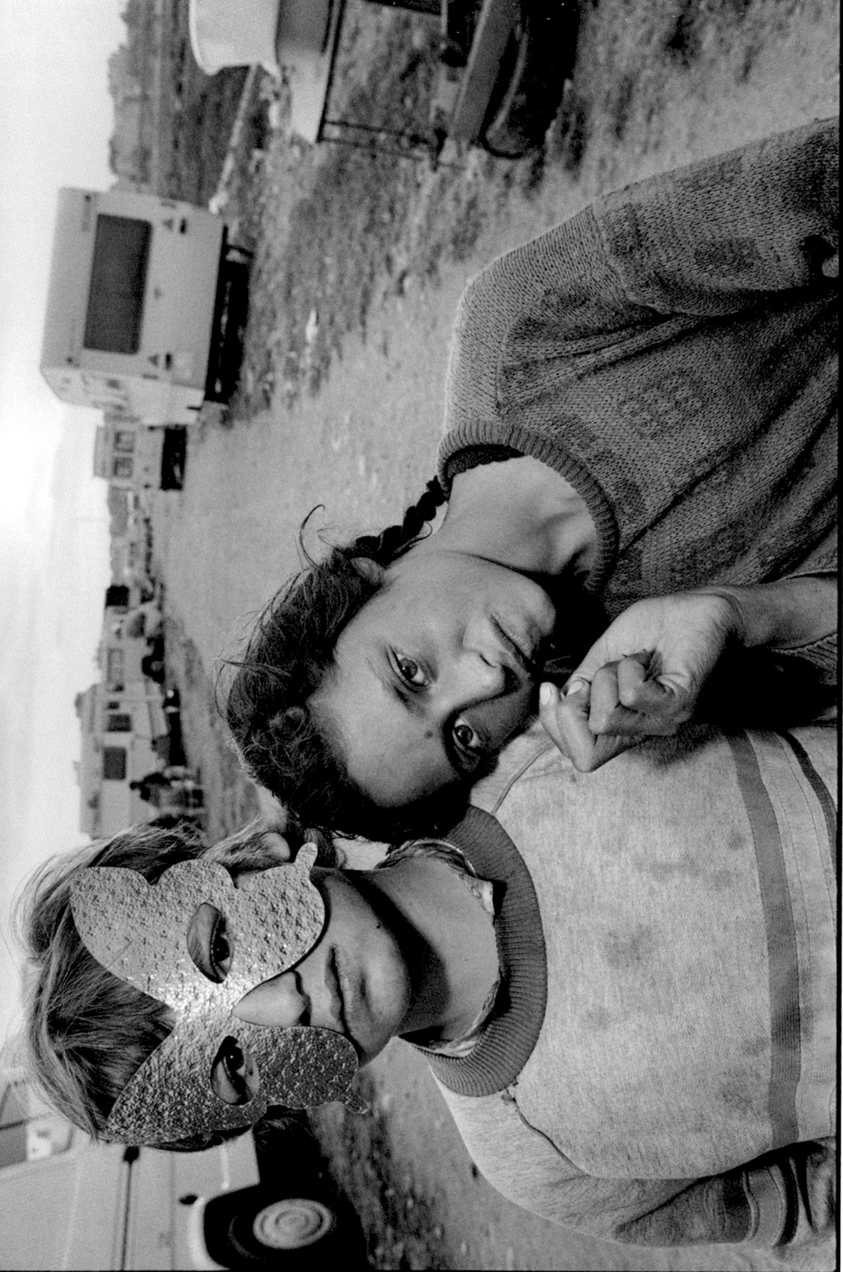

47. Pro-Vietnam War demonstrator with his mother.
New York, 1968 .

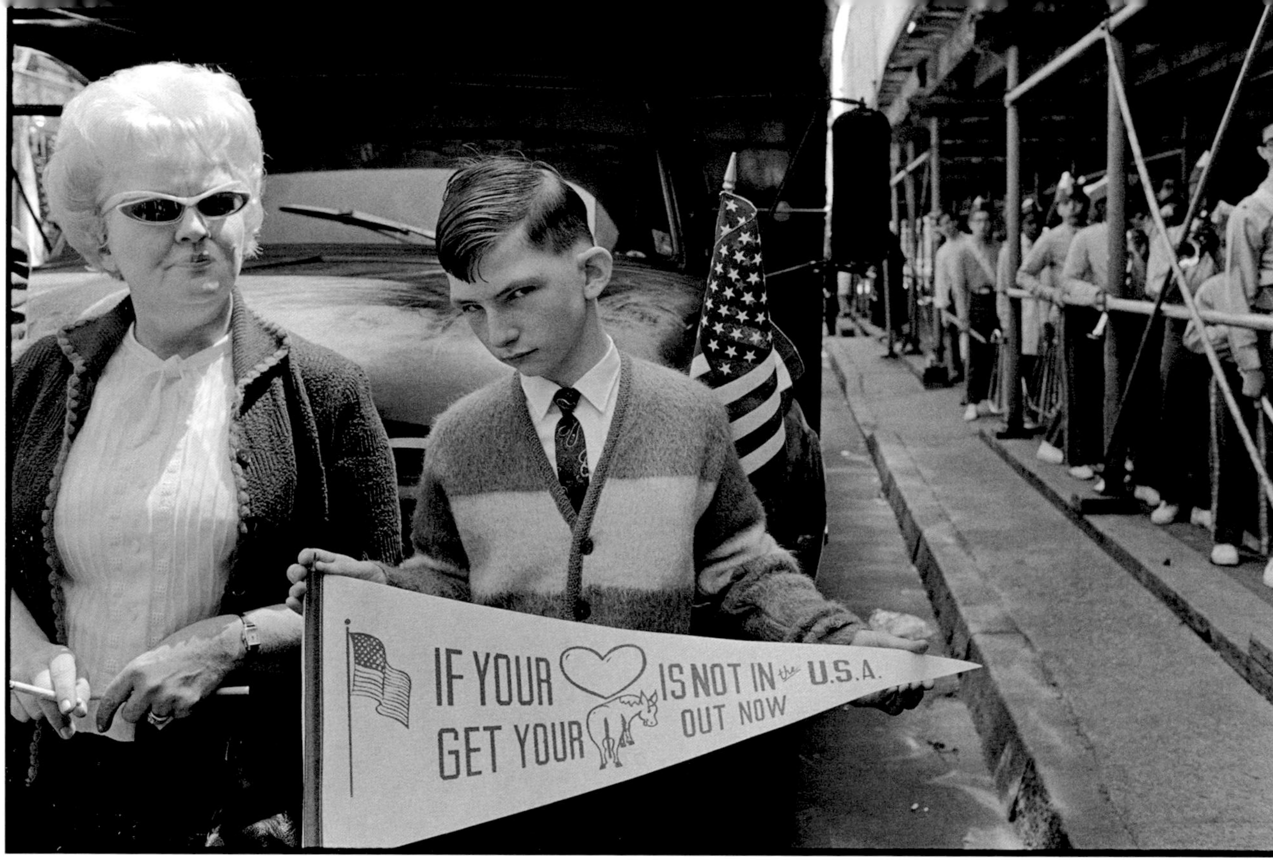
IF YOUR ♥ IS NOT IN the U.S.A.
GET YOUR 🐴 OUT NOW

48. Young bull riders with dollar bills
at Boerne Rodeo. Texas, 1991.

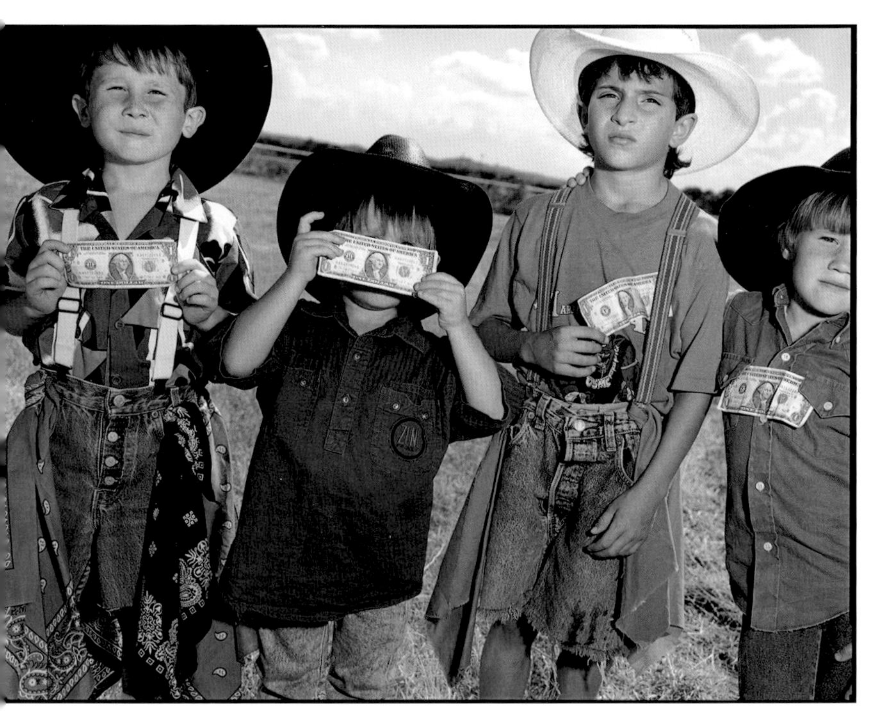

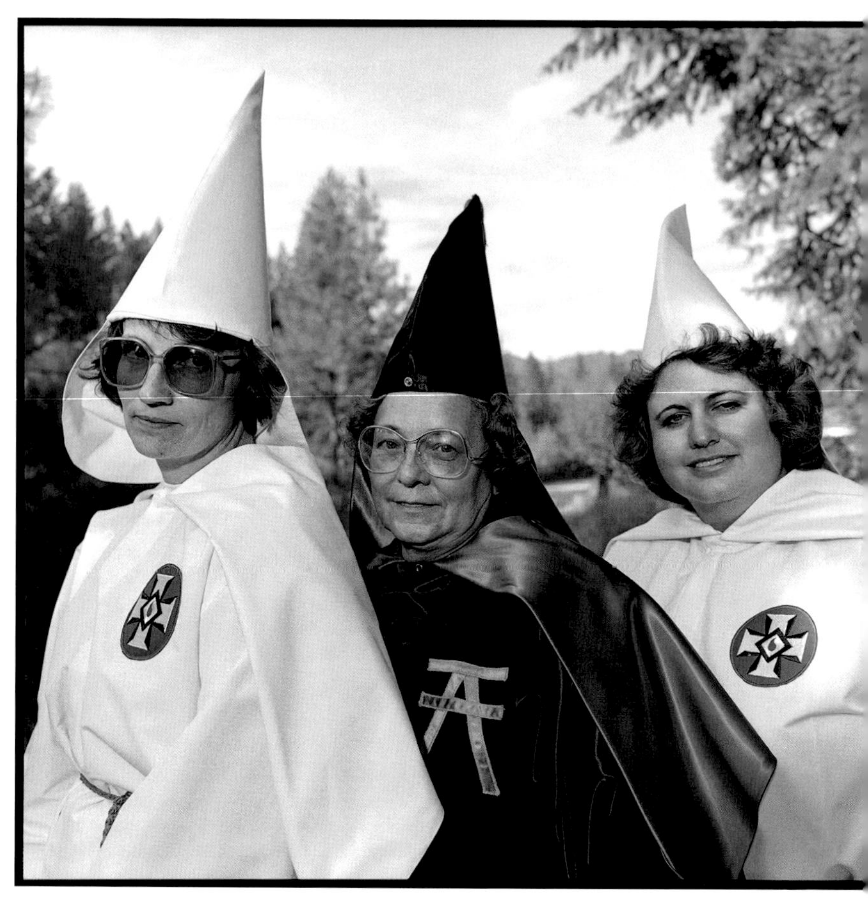

49. Wives of the Aryan Nations.
Hayden Lake, Idaho, 1986.

50. Father and son at the Aryan Nations Congress.
Hayden Lake, Idaho, 1986.

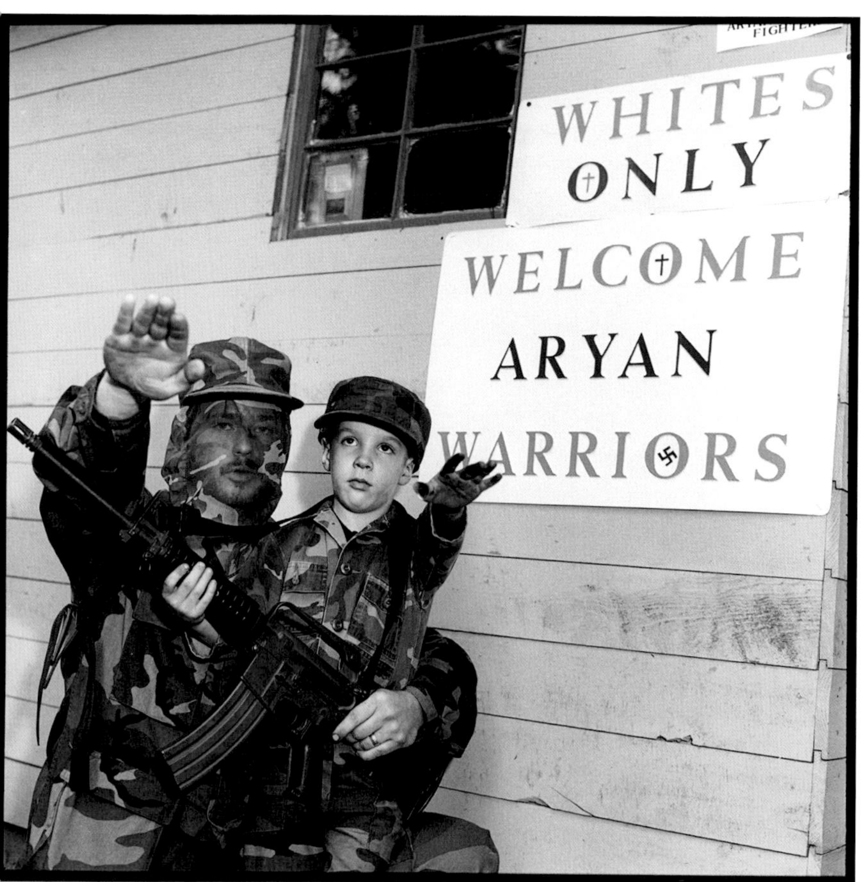
ARYAN
FIGHTER
WHITES
ONLY
WELCOME
ARYAN
WARRIORS

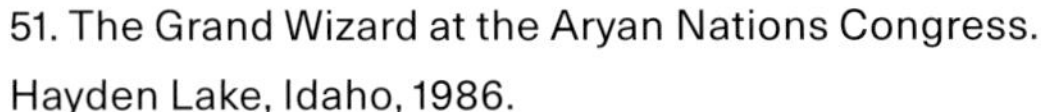

51. The Grand Wizard at the Aryan Nations Congress.
Hayden Lake, Idaho, 1986.

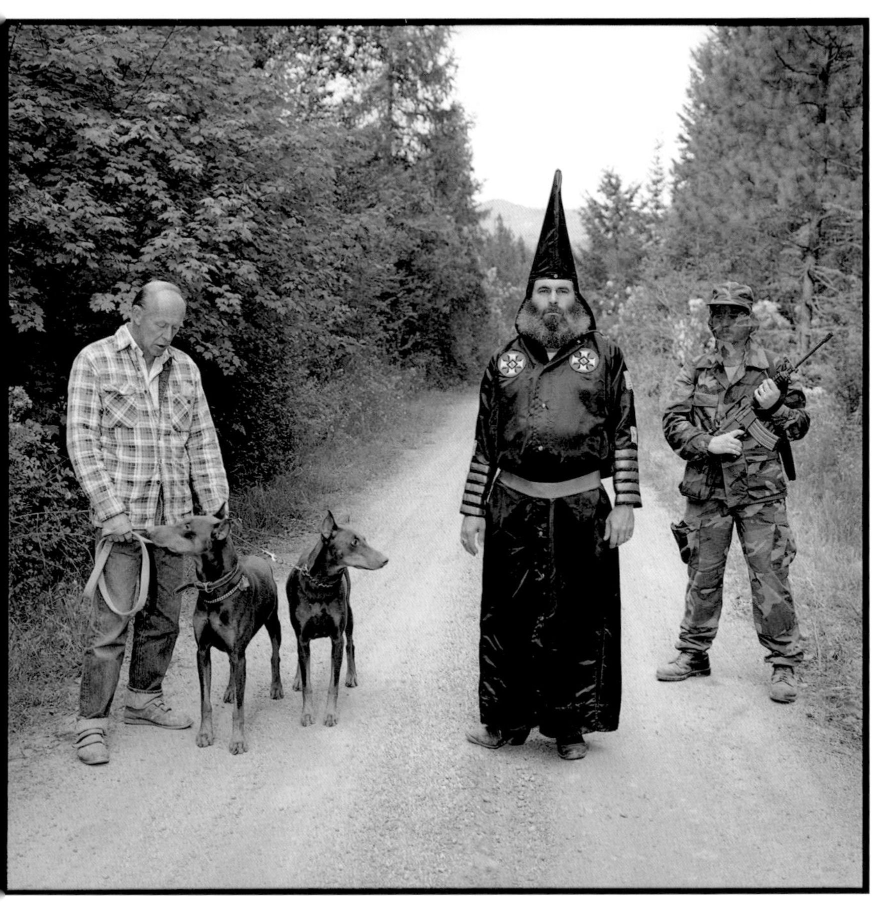

52. Feminist demonstration. New York, 1970.

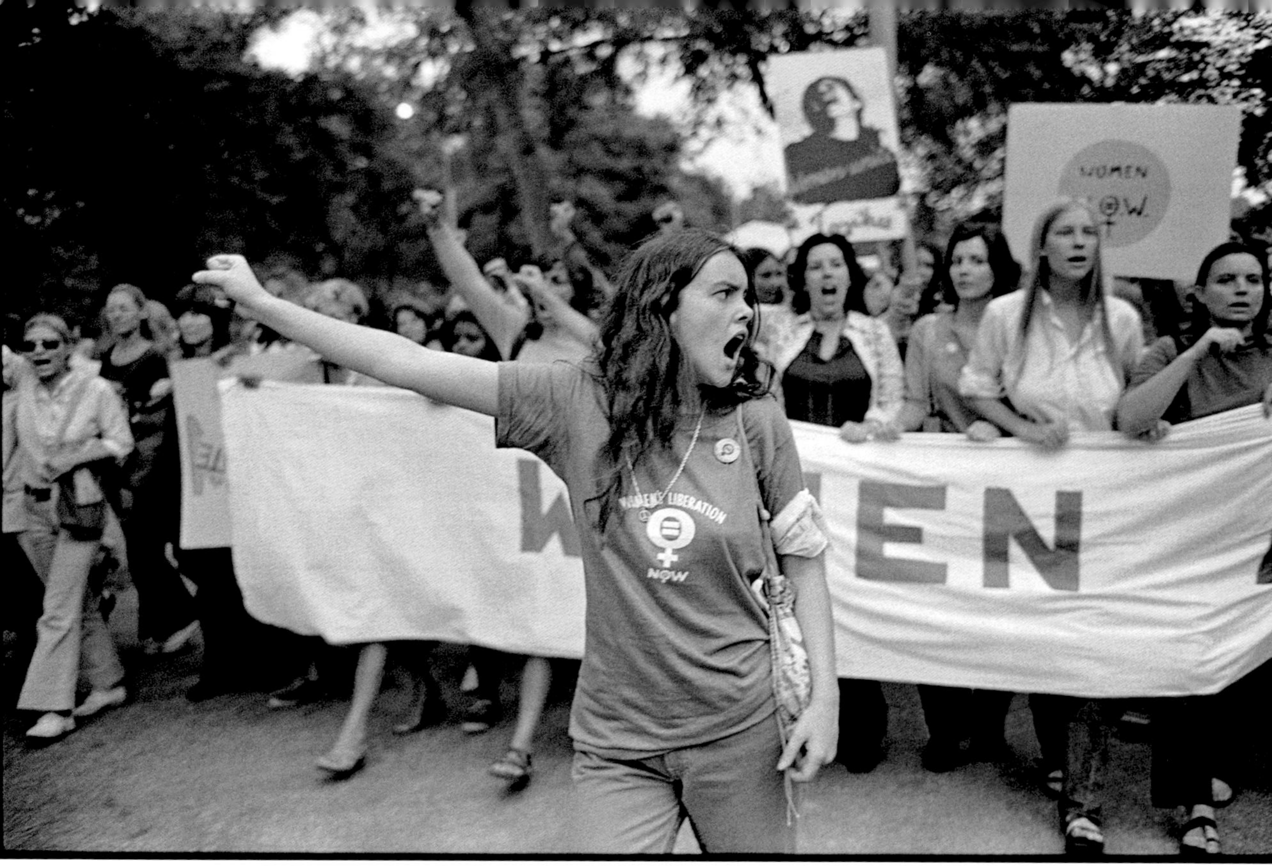

WOMEN'S LIBERATION
NOW
WOMEN
NOW
WOMEN

53. Acadian wedding. Lafayette, Louisiana, 1972.

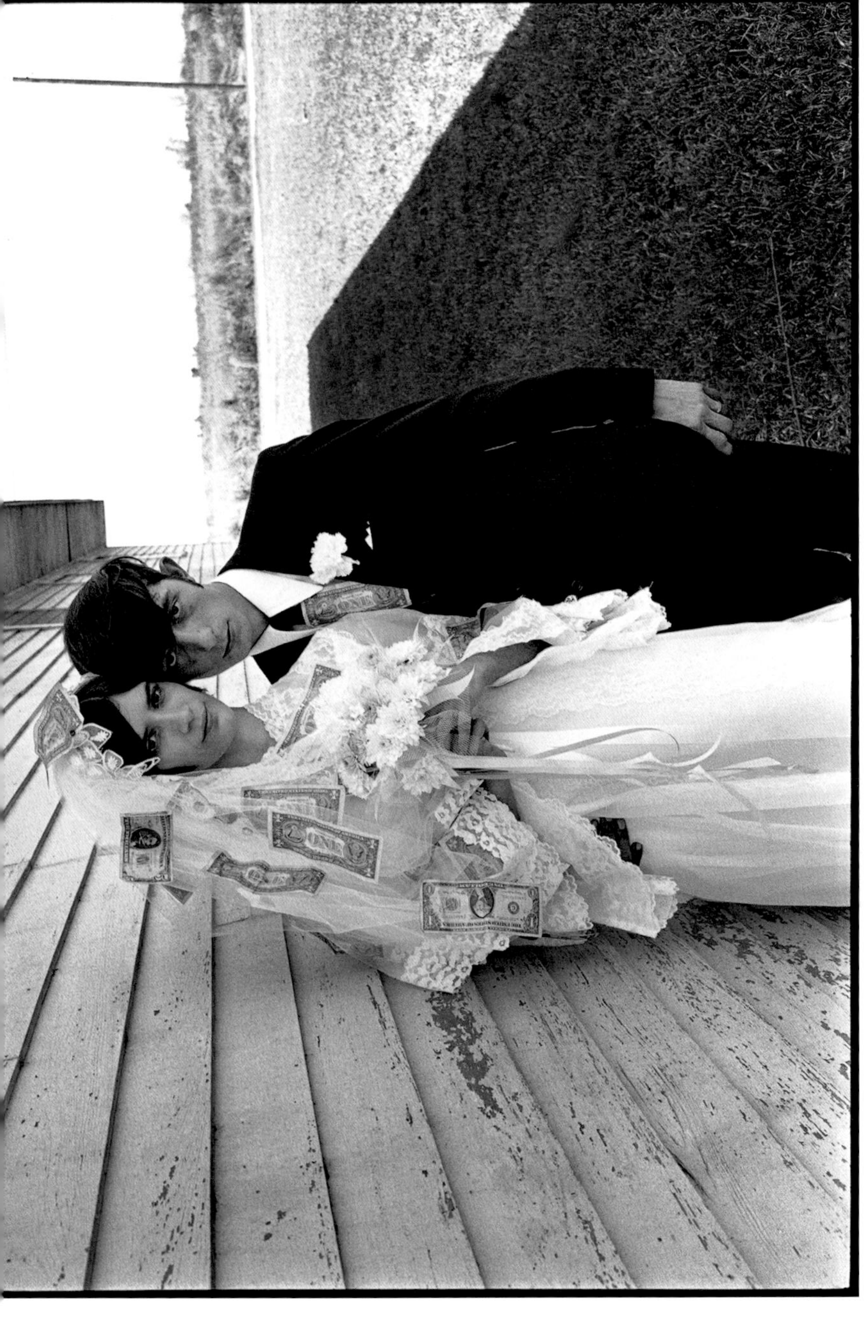

54. Elise Collins in costume. Union, South Carolina, 1995.

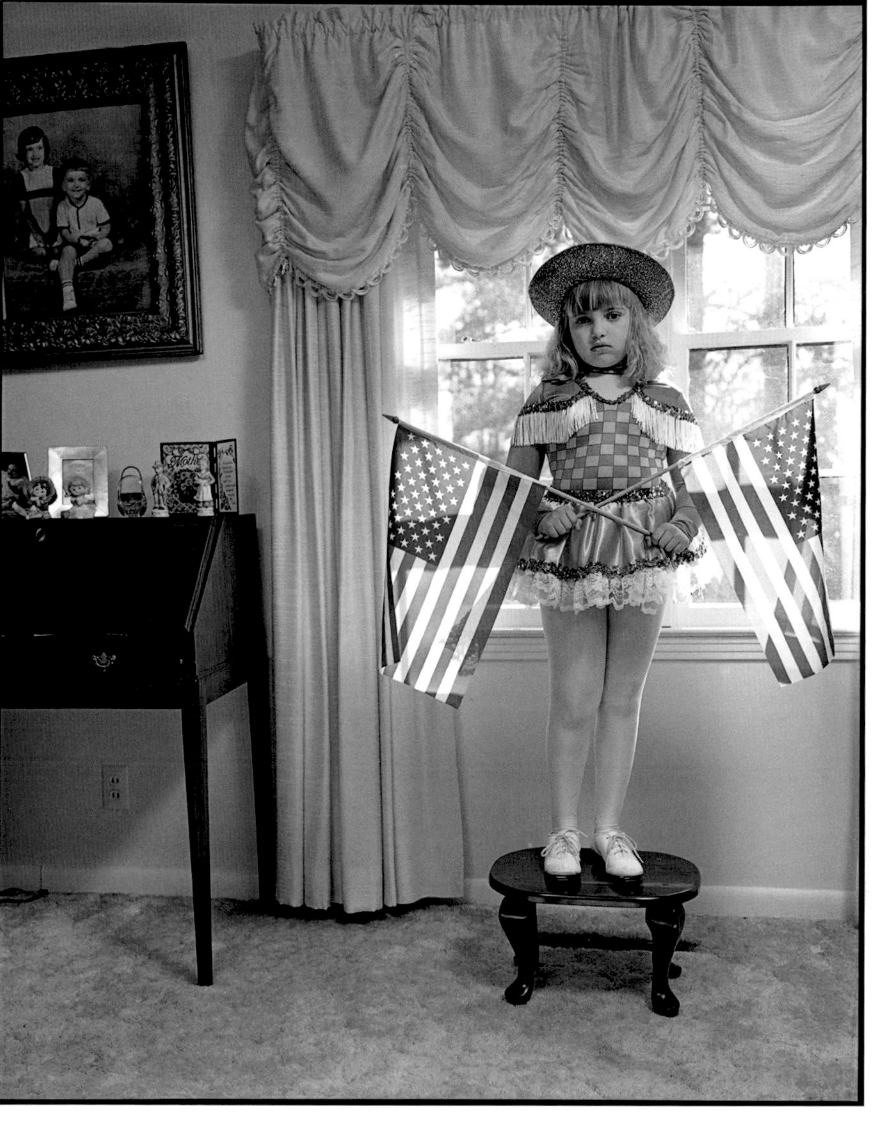

55. Jerry Hill and Margaret Sell at the Hilton Hotel
Dance Showcase. Boca Raton, Florida, 1993.

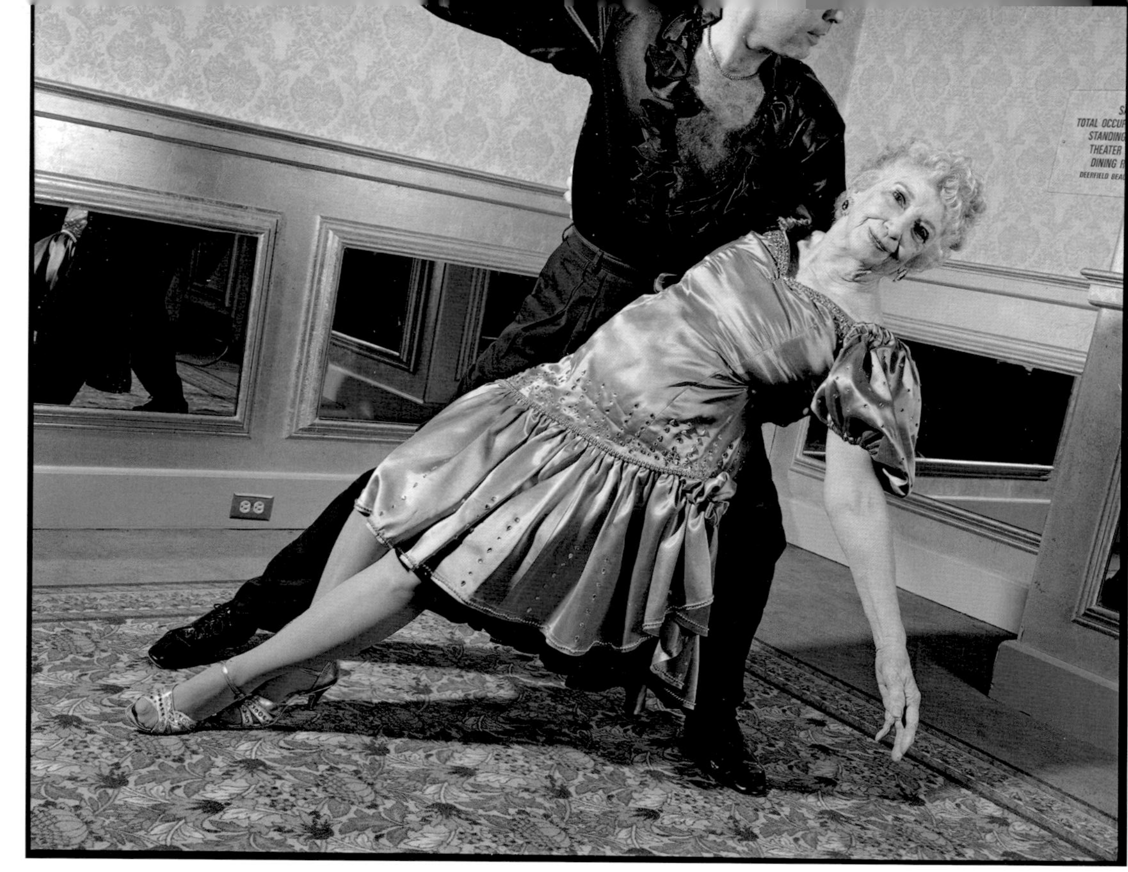

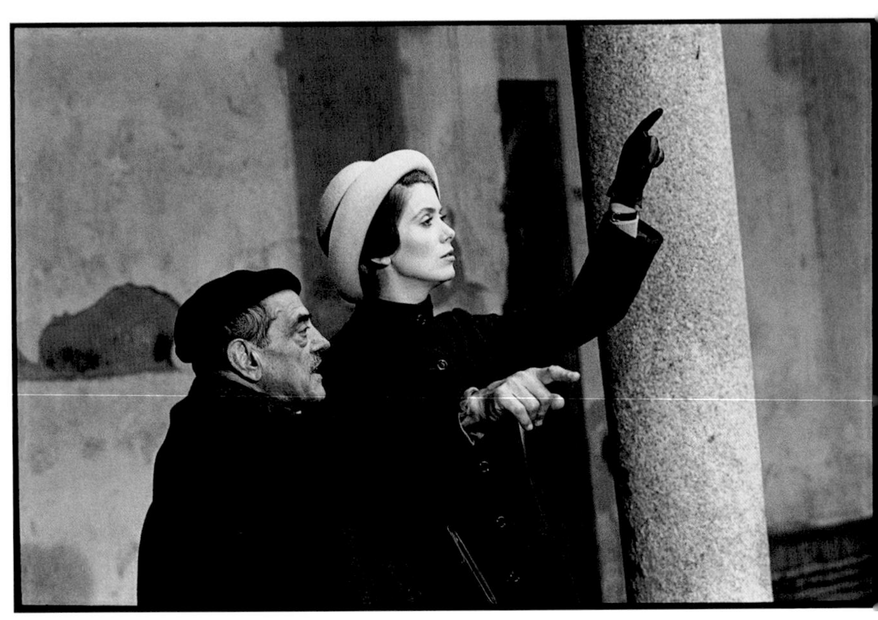

56. Luis Buñuel directs Catherine Deneuve
in Tristana. Toledo, Spain, 1969.

57. Federico Fellini with a bullhorn during the
shooting of *Fellini Satyricon*. Rome, 1969.

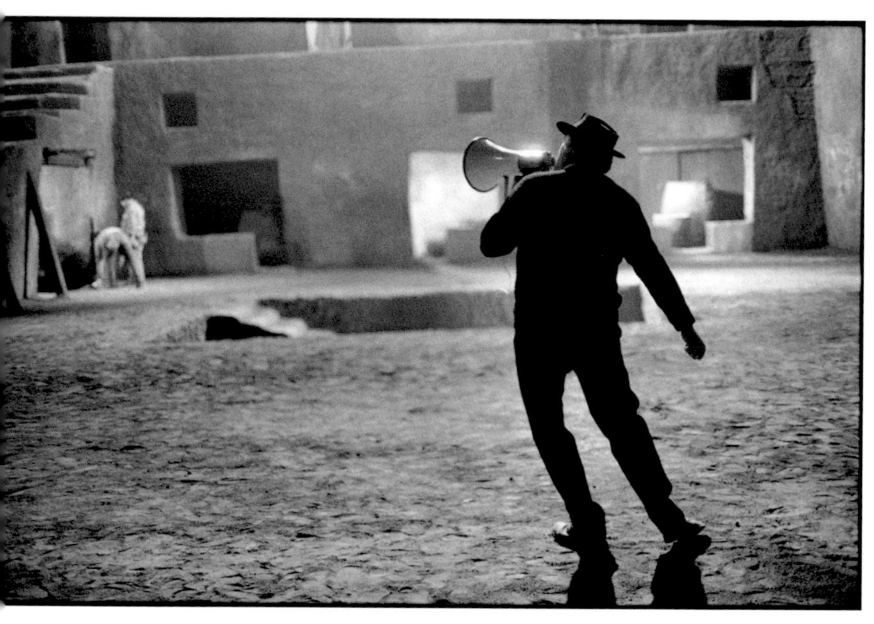

58. Dennis Hopper peering through an American
flag during the shooting of Francis Ford Coppola's
Apocalypse Now. Pagsanjan, Philippines, 1976.

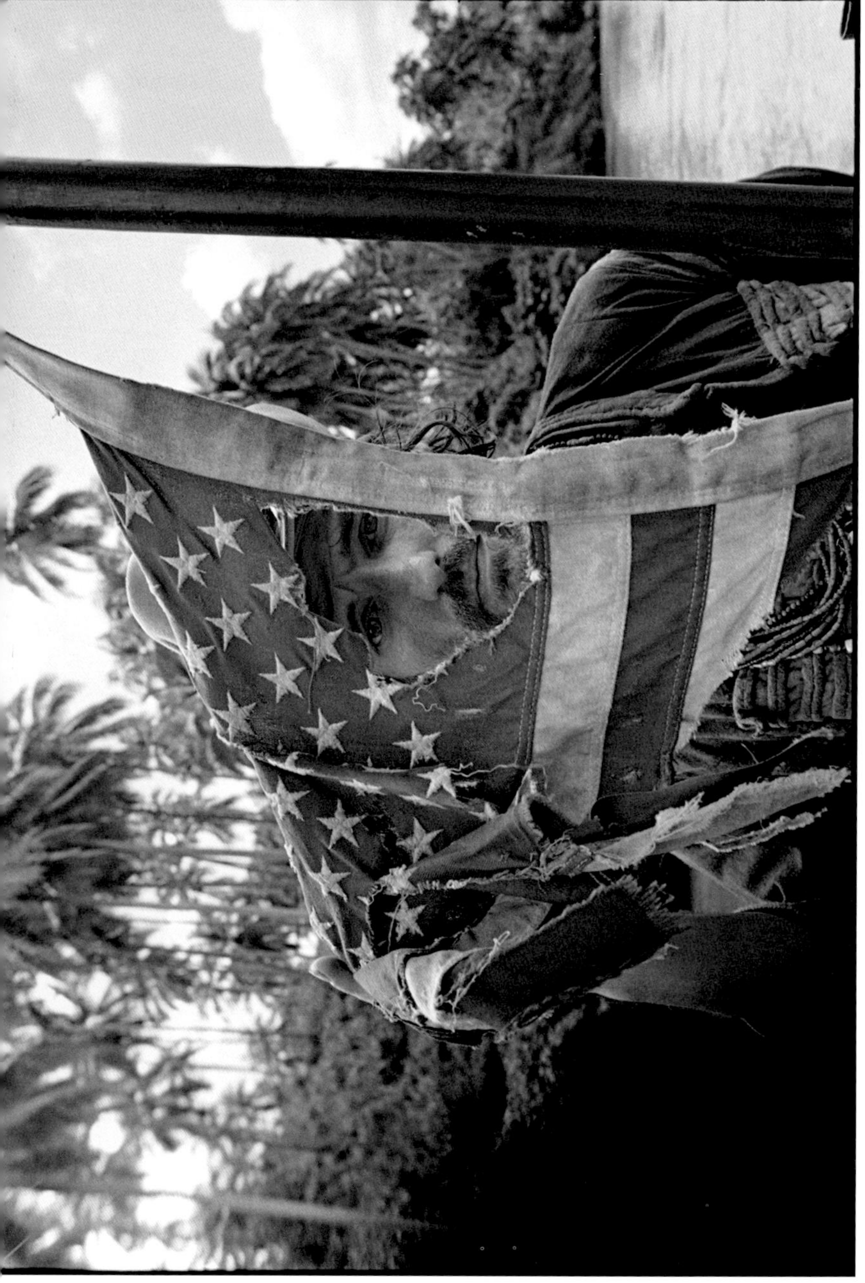

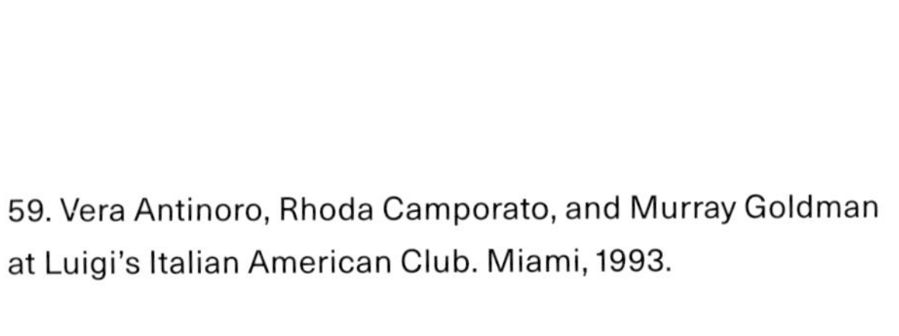

59. Vera Antinoro, Rhoda Camporato, and Murray Goldman
at Luigi's Italian American Club. Miami, 1993.

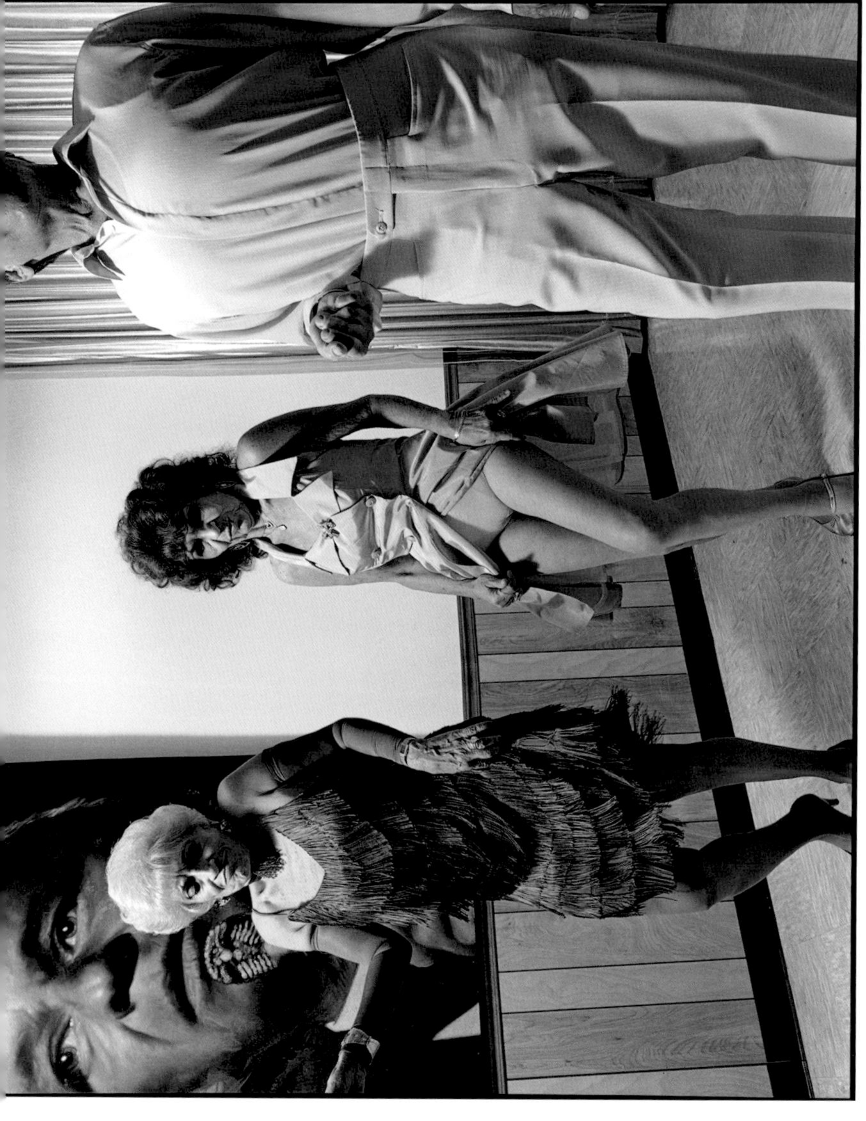

60. Sue Gallo Baugher and Faye Gallo at the Twins
Days Festival. Twinsburg, Ohio, 1998.

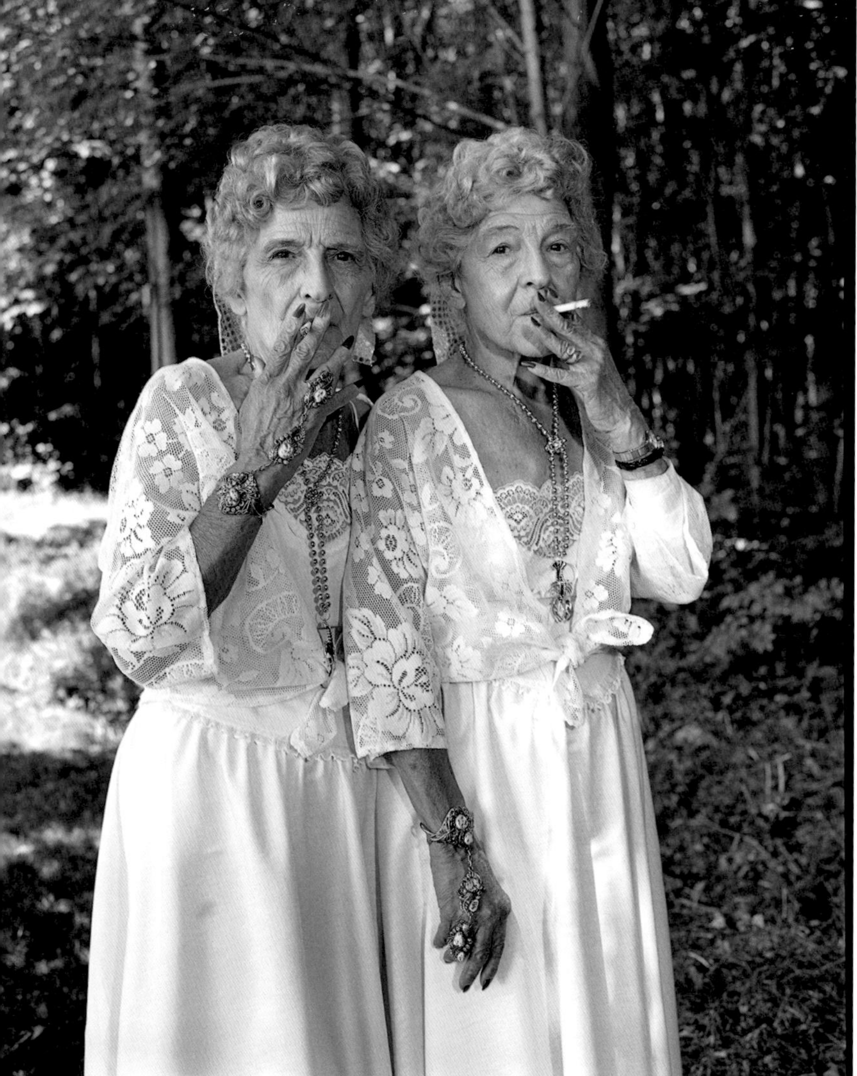

61. Brooke and Billy at Gibbs High School prom.
St. Petersburg, Florida, 1986.

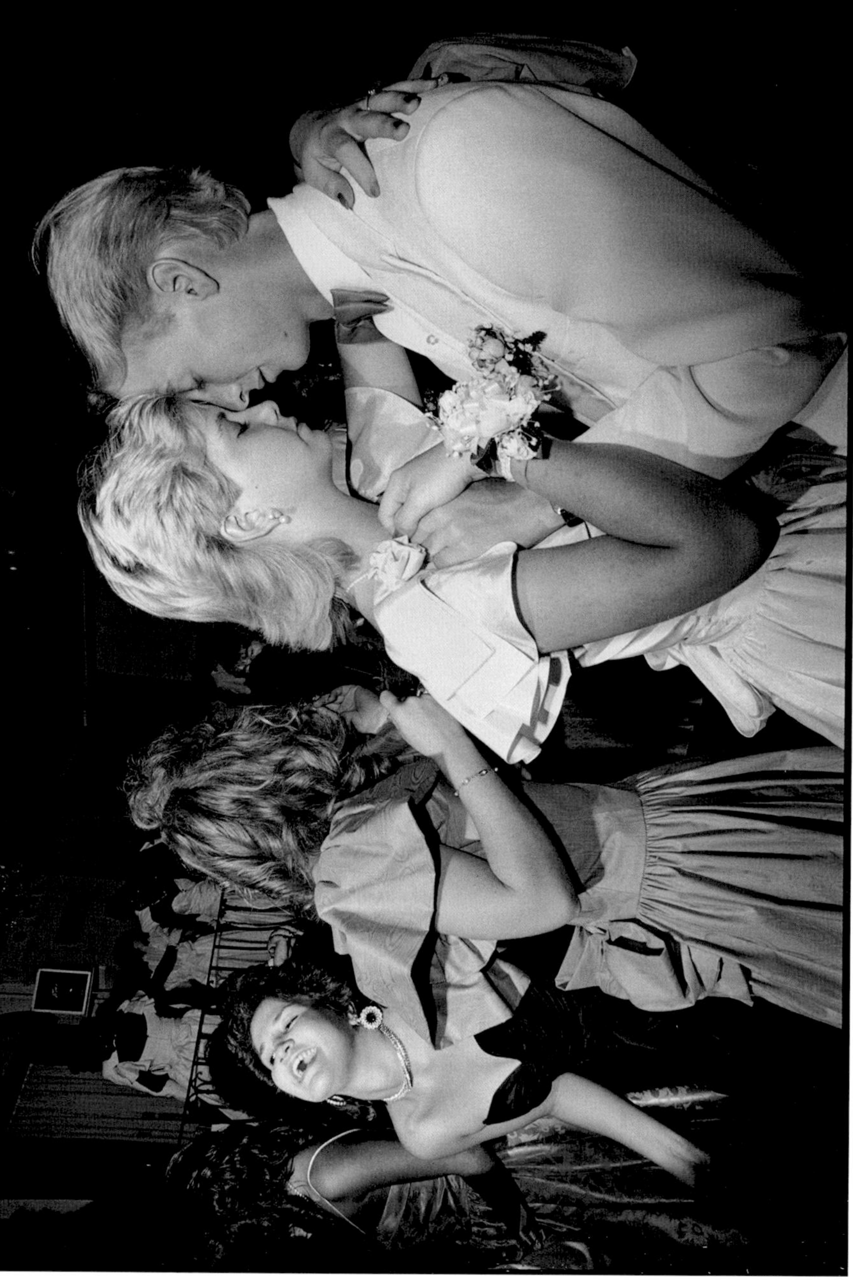

62. Lourdes at a children's fashion show.
Miami Beach, 1986.

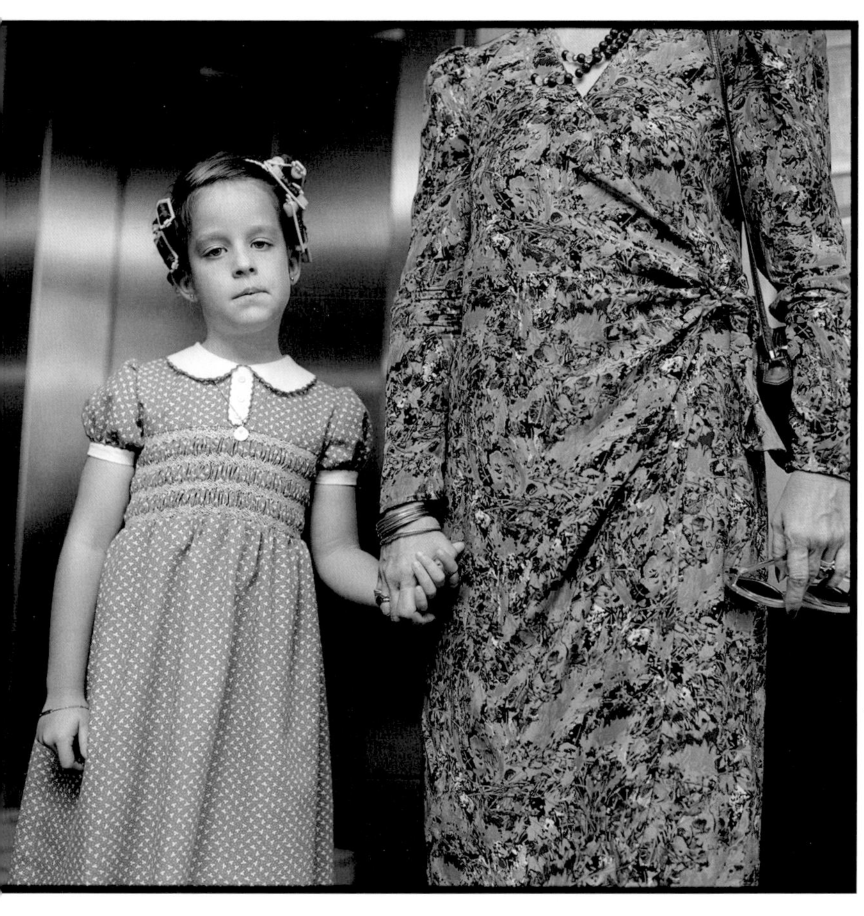

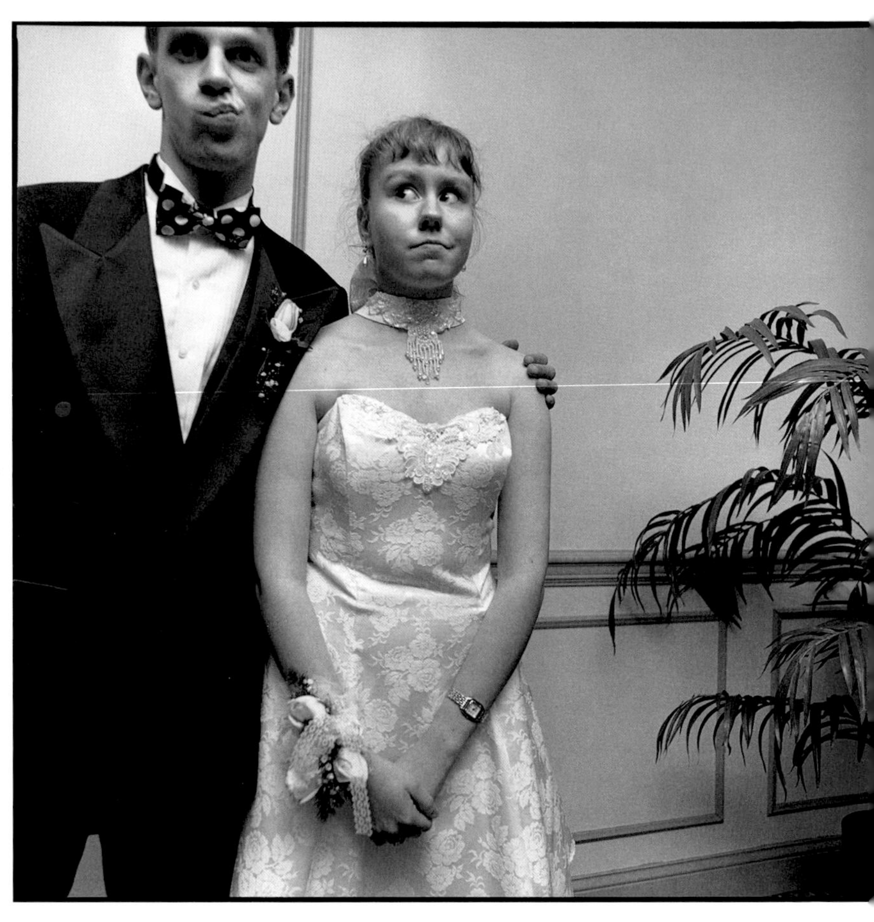

63. Andy Monz and Tricia Rorison at the
Peabody High School prom. Pittsburgh, 1995.

64. Happy New Year couple at home.
Miami Beach, 1979.

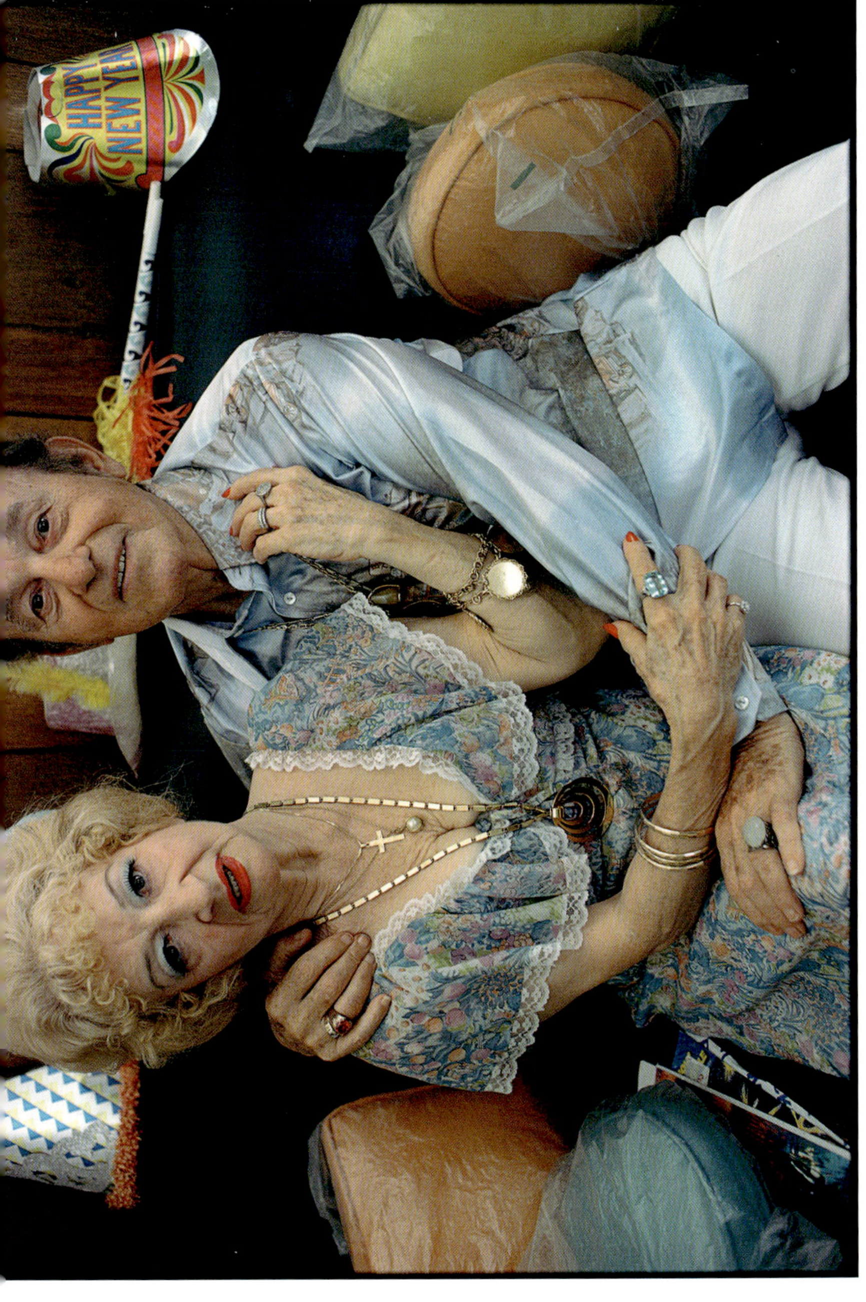

HAPPY
NEW YEAR

65. Dancing woman at senior citizens center.
Miami Beach, 1979.

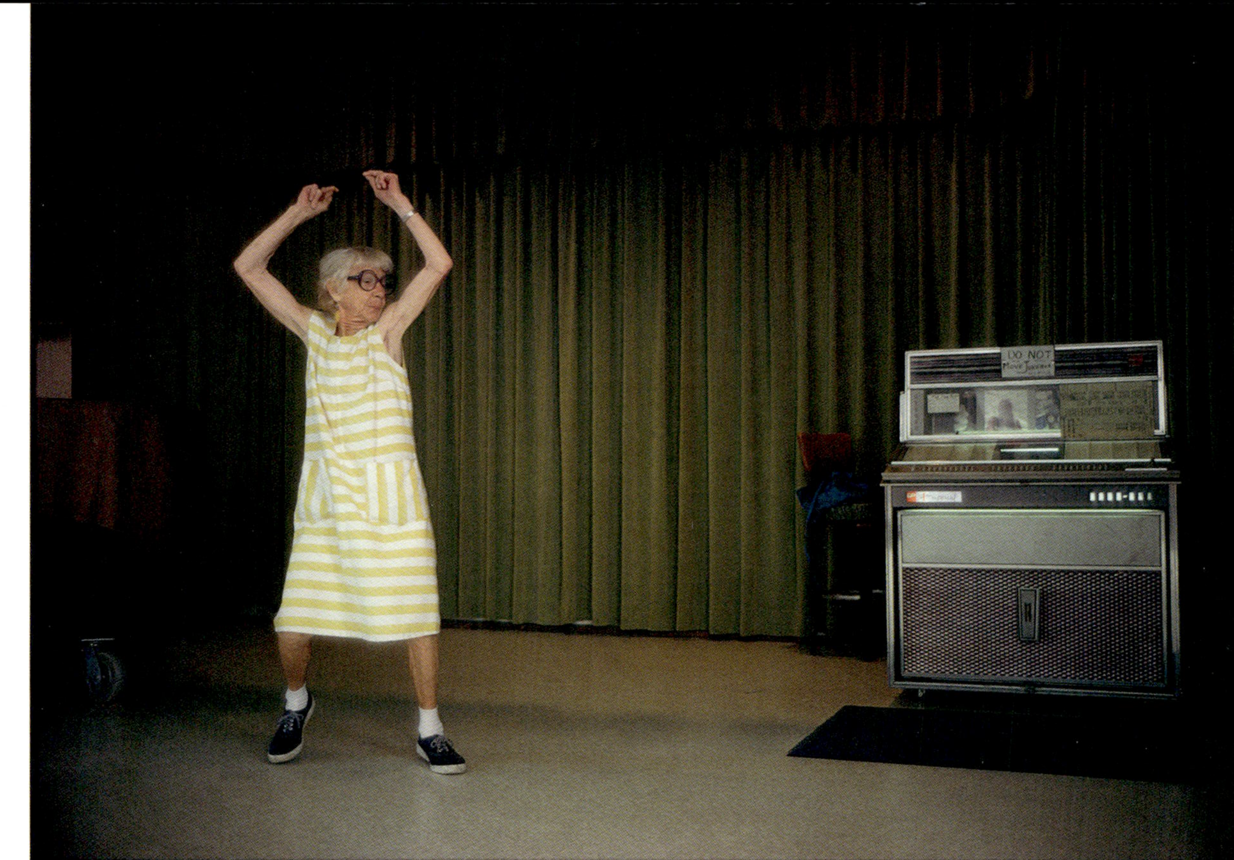
DO NOT
Move Jukebox

66. Water exercise group. St. Petersburg, Florida, 1986.

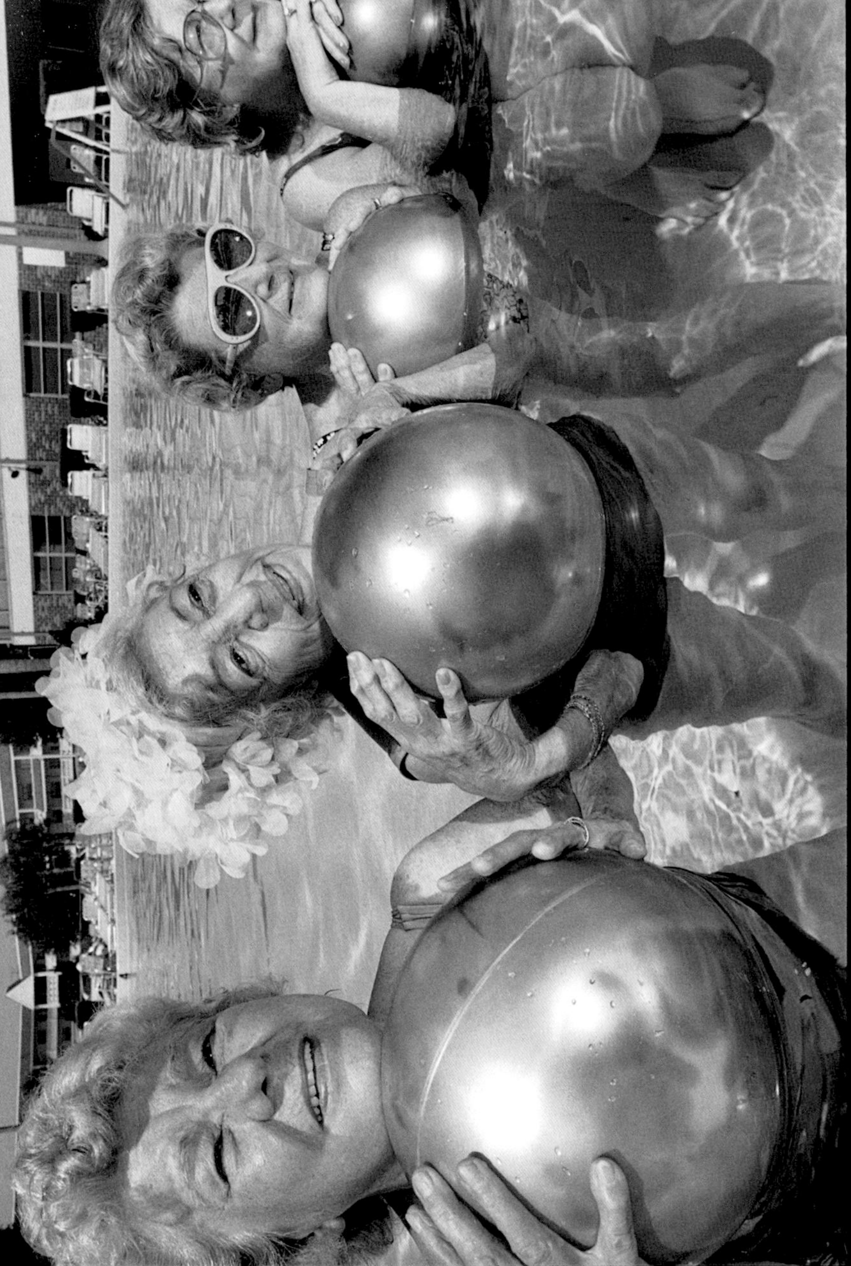

67. Christina Ricci in her dressing room on the set of Tim
Burton's *Sleepy Hollow*. Shepperton Studios, England, 1999.

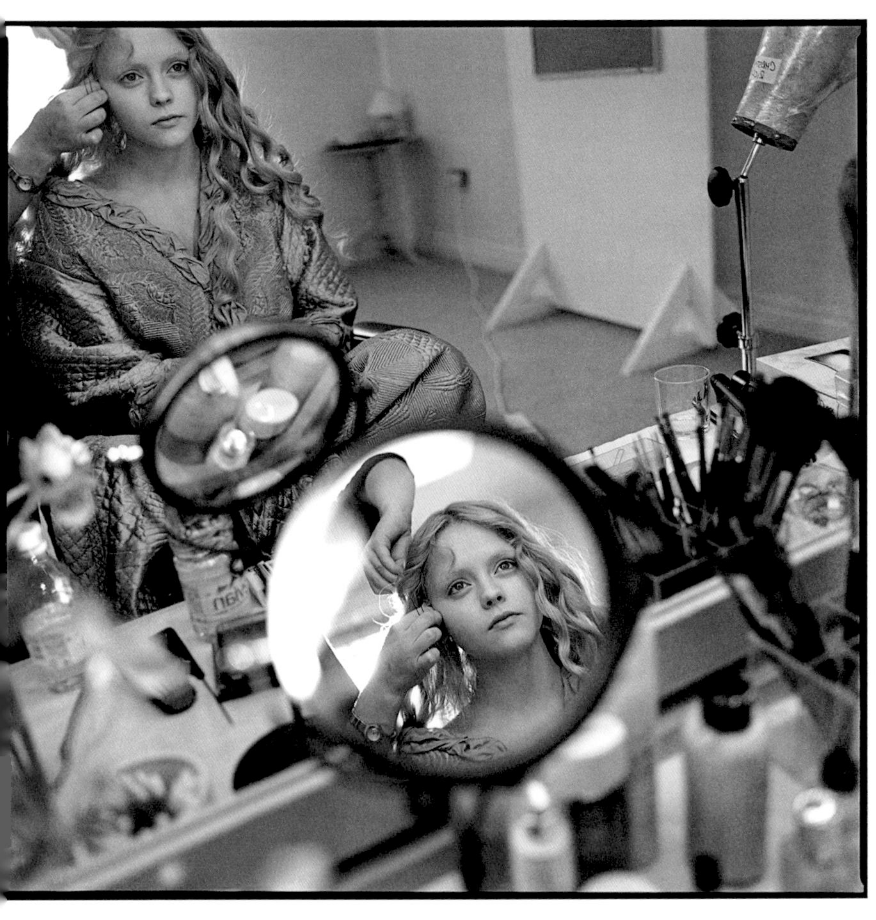

68. Kissing in a bar. New York, 1977.

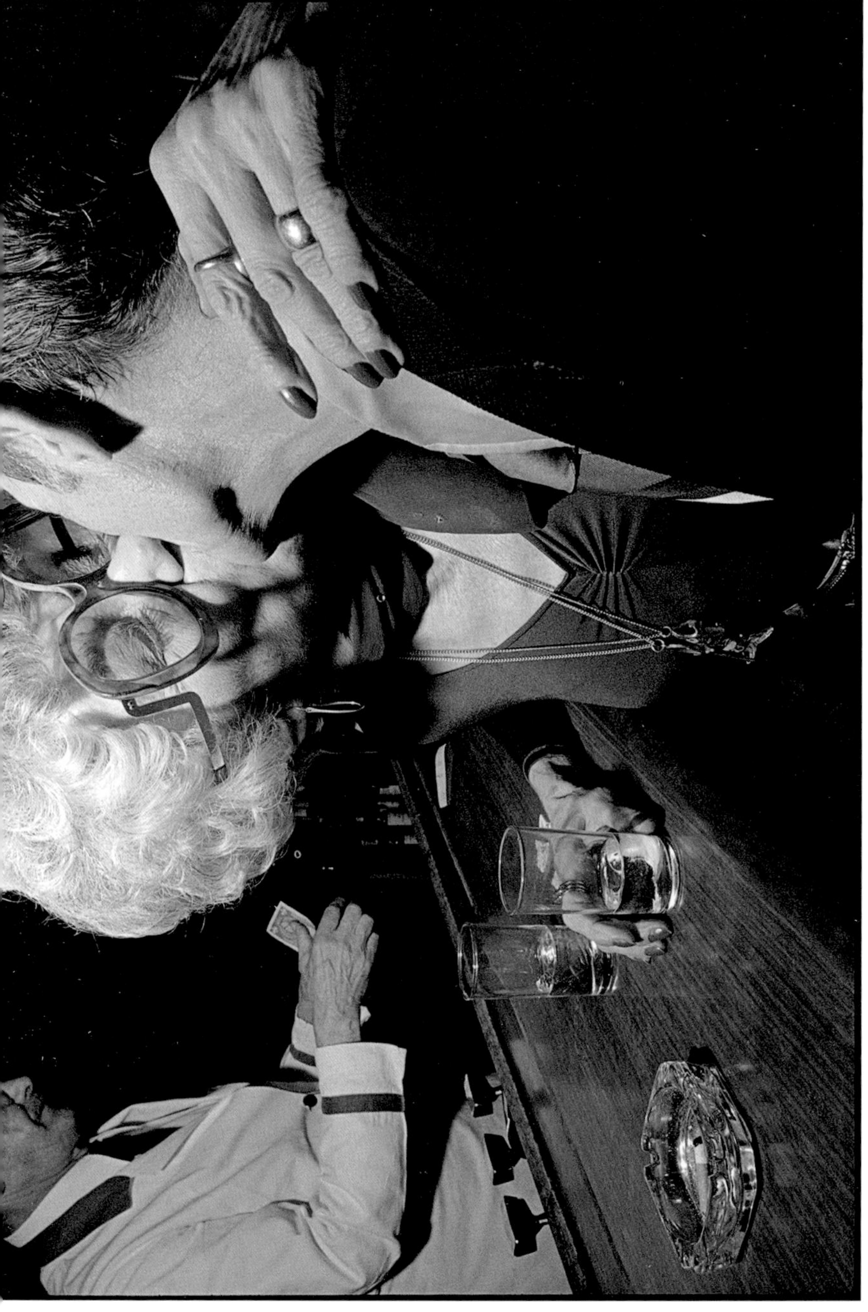

69. Women's bar. Upper East Side, New York, 1977.

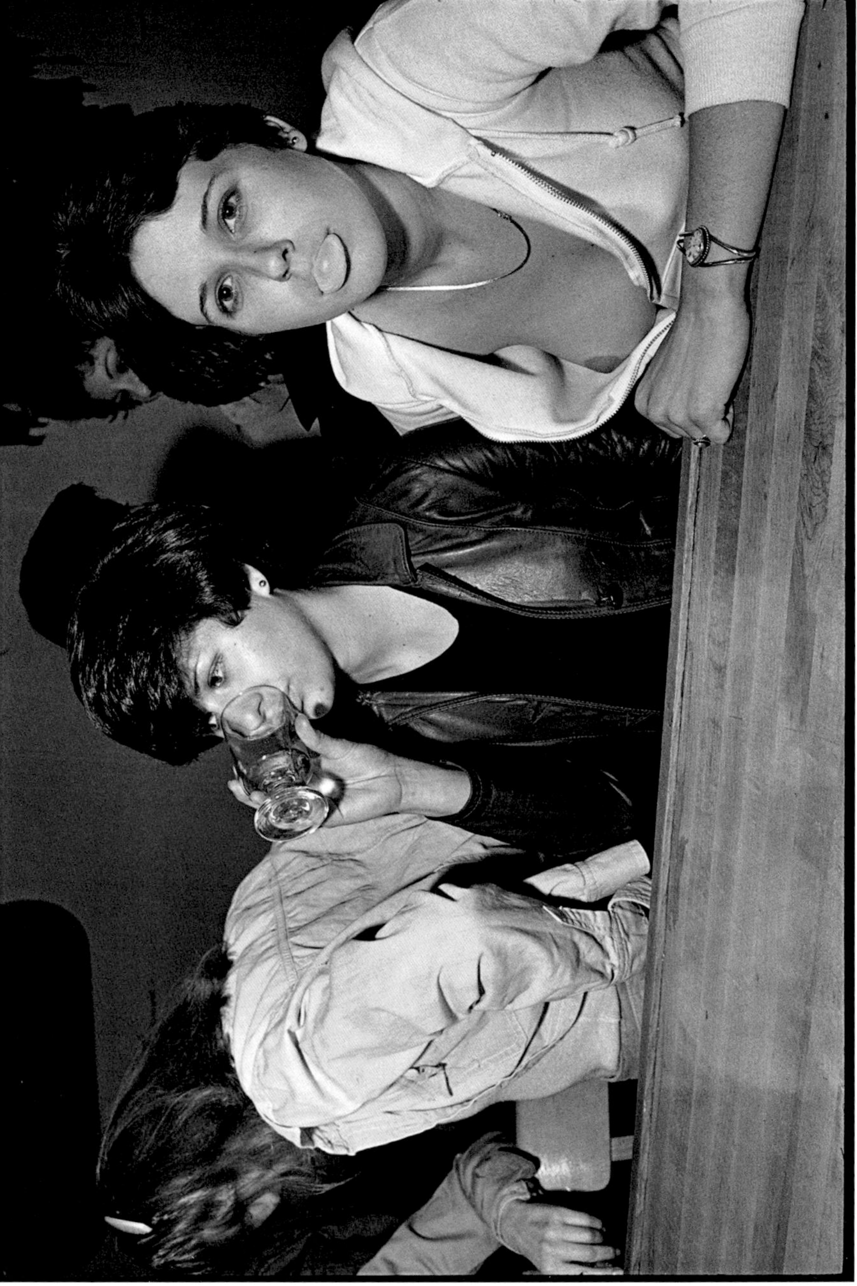

70. Girl jumping over a wall in Central Park.
New York, ca. 1967.

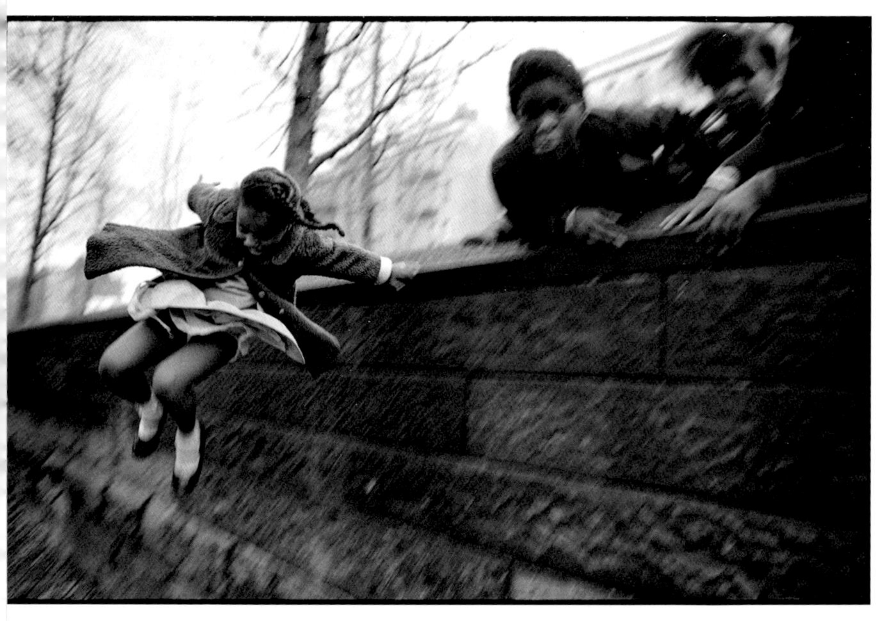

Selected exhibitions

1976 *Bars*, The Photographer's Gallery, London.

1977 *Ward 81*, Santa Barbara Museum of Art, Santa Barbara, CA.

1981 *Falkland Road*, Castelli Graphics, New York.

1985 *Mother Teresa and Calcutta*, Allen Street Gallery, Dallas, TX.

1987 *Mary Ellen Mark: Photographs*, University of Oklahoma, Museum of Art, Norman, OK.

1988 *Portraits*, Photography Gallery, Santa Monica College, Santa Monica, CA.

1988 *America*, Pasadena Art Center, Pasadena, CA.

1991 *Indian Circus: Platinum Prints*, Castelli Graphics, New York.

1992 *Mary Ellen Mark: 25 Years*, International Center for Photography, New York.

2000 *Strange Moments*, Howard Greenberg Gallery, New York.
American Odyssey, Kulturhuset, Stockholm.

2001–2007 *American Odyssey*, European touring exhibition.

2003 *Twins*, Marianne Boesky Gallery / Kennedy Boesky Photographs, New York.

2004 *Twins*, Fotomuseum Den Haag, The Hague.

2007 *Undrabörn: Extraordinary Child*, National Museum of Iceland, Reykjavik.

2008 *Prom*, Festival of the Photograph, Charlottesville, VA

2009 *Indian Circus*, Howard Greenberg Gallery, New York.

2012 *Prom*, Philadelphia Museum of Art, Philadelphia, PA.

2014 *Man and Beast*, Wittliff Collections, Texas State University, San Marcos, TX.

2015 *Tiny: Streetwise Revisited*, Norton Museum of Art, West Palm Beach, FL.

2016 *Attitude*, Howard Greenberg Gallery, New York.

2020–2021 *The Lives of Women*, Kulturhuset Stadsteatern, Stockholm; Fotofestival Lenzburg, Switzerland; Fundación Foto Colectania, Barcelona.

2021 *Girlhood*, National Museum of Women in the Arts, Washington DC.

2022 *Remarkable Women*, Leica Gallery, Boston.
The Lives of Women, Maison de la Photographie Robert Doisneau, Gentilly.

2023–2024 *Encounters*, C/O Berlin.

2024 *The Lives of Women*, Städtische Museen, Heilbronn, Germany.
Encounters, Les Rencontres d'Arles.

The Photofile series is the original English-language edition of the Photo Poche collection. It was first published between 1986 and 1992 by the Centre National de la Photographie, Paris, with the support of the French Ministry of Culture. Robert Delpire (1926–2017) was the creator of the series and its managing editor until 2017.

General editor: Géraldine Lay and Anne Morin
Assistant editor: Marie Constant

Series design by Matthew Young

Translated from the French by Ruth Sharman

First published in the United Kingdom in 2024 by
Thames & Hudson Ltd, 181A High Holborn, London WC1V 7QX

First published in the United States of America in 2024 by
Thames & Hudson Inc., 500 Fifth Avenue, New York, New York 10110

British Library Cataloguing-in-Publication Data
A catalogue record for this book is available from the British Library

Library of Congress Control Number 2024934759.

ISBN 978-0-500-41125-4

Printed and bound in Italy

Be the first to know about our new releases, exclusive content and author events by visiting
thamesandhudson.com
thamesandhudsonusa.com
thamesandhudson.com.au